Peter Meyer

❧❧❧❦❦❦

With a Foreword by
Harold Taylor

AWARDING COLLEGE CREDIT FOR NON-COLLEGE LEARNING

Jossey-Bass Publishers
San Francisco • Washington • London • 1975

AWARDING COLLEGE CREDIT FOR NON-COLLEGE LEARNING
A Guide to Current Practices
    Peter Meyer

Copyright © 1975 by: Jossey-Bass, Inc., Publishers
                          615 Montgomery Street
                          San Francisco, California 94111
                                    &
                          Jossey-Bass Limited
                          3 Henrietta Street
                          London WC2E 8LU

Library of Congress Catalogue Card Number LC 74-28918

International Standard Book Number ISBN 0-87589-254-X

Manufactured in the United States of America

JACKET DESIGN BY WILLI BAUM

FIRST EDITION

Code 7504

The Jossey-Bass
Series in Higher Education

Foreword

If you want to ride a horse, dance a jig, climb a mountain, build a boat, write a novel, study history, think intelligently, become educated, a certain amount of instruction in a class in the subject will be useful—perhaps for two or three sessions. After that you will need to get a horse, start dancing, climbing, building, writing, thinking, and educating on your own. Otherwise you will not have learned what you need to know, that is, how in fact to do the thing you have set out to learn to do. To learn to do something it is necessary to practice it.

Although this is astonishingly clear as a general proposition, the entire American educational system is built on the opposite principle, that learning is done only through instruction and intervention by a teacher who explains, describes, instructs, and then certifies that the learner was present in a class while the explanations and descriptions were being given.

So prevalent is this view of learning and so pernicious its effect in educational institutions that it has taken years of struggle, research, and rebellion to return to the simple clarity of the original truth about education and to put its consequences into practice. The idea that knowledge stems from experience and that knowing is an activity of the one who knows has a respectable ancestry in the British empirical philosophers, the psychology of William James, the views of the existentialists, and the educational theories of Alfred North Whitehead and John Dewey, among others. The idea also has the advantage of being continually affirmed in the experience of anyone who has ever learned anything.

The present book by Peter Meyer, in its broadest terms, is a practical guide to the way the relation between knowledge and experience can be made explicit in the American system of higher education. If we are interested in knowing what an individual has actually learned rather than what courses he has taken in an educational institution, a whole new set of practices must be developed to assess the results of all forms of experiences which are assumed to be educative. When you strip education of all its formalities and institutional practices, what it comes down to is a set of experiences which affect the learner in one way or another. If the experiences are truly educative, it does not matter whether they happened inside or outside an educational institution. It is a question of what has been learned and how to assess the results.

The need for radical alternatives to the present system has been obvious for many years. The experimental colleges of the early 1930s and 1940s—Antioch, Bennington, Sarah Lawrence, Goddard—now joined by others among the more conventional colleges, have investigated such alternatives and produced systems of their own. As one who had been educated in the British system and was suddenly confronted in his first teaching assignment with the American pattern of academic credits, tests, grades, grade-point averages, course requirements, lectures, and the rest, I found the American system simple-minded and intellectually inhibiting to students and teachers alike. I was asked to give examinations in which I did not believe and to assign grades which measured little more than student competence in writing and taking examinations.

Before that first confrontation more than thirty-five years ago, I had no idea what academic credits were, except that three of them were awarded for spending fifteen weeks, three times a week, with one separate discussion session each week, in my classes in philosophy. After suitable enquiries I learned that academic credits had originally been invented to handle the problem of fitting the student into the proper level of study in a college to which he might transfer, and that other than this bookkeeping function, on the basis of which a degree could eventually be granted, academic credits had no educational use.

Nor was there any inclination among my informants—registrars, admissions officers, or faculty members—to face the fact that possession of a small hoard of academic credits did not mean that the student who had stored them away was actually in possession of knowledge in the field in which the credits were awarded. It was an entire system in which grades, tests, averages, and units of credit all went together. No one seemed to feel that college education could be carried on in any other way or that there was any point in trying.

Although I discovered that there were ways of getting around the system while teaching in it, it was not until I arrived at Sarah Lawrence College, where a complete reversal of educational conventions was the basis of the program, that I learned at first hand about the virtues and problems of an alternative and progressive system. At Sarah Lawrence there were no academic credits, grades, examinations, or required courses. There were few lectures; there was widespread student involvement in making educational policy, with each student taking an active part in putting together a personal curriculum and making decisions about what should be studied and in what way. The experimental colleges were experimenting, some of them more fully than Sarah Lawrence, with a combination of work experience and college study which broke down the isolation of academic studies from the social and cultural reality which gave them meaning. In this case it was not a question of considering what academic credit could be given for work experience, but of building a new conception of the whole process of education and of considering the place of non-college work in that process.

The year I arrived at Sarah Lawrence (1945) the experimental colleges had already proved what they set out to prove in these matters—the validity of work experience in a college program. It was the year that Sarah Lawrence, having already established a nursery school as part of the experimental program in teaching and research in child psychology, appointed its first director of field work. There had grown up such a variety of field projects and programs, in community agencies, action research, field experience in the arts, field trips, and practical work of all kinds, that an office had to be organized to make the arrangements and keep track of the results. There was no division between academic studies and practical experience. It was assumed by the college and by most of the faculty members and students that the two went together.

Whenever it was necessary to award academic credit—for example, in the case of subject matter requirements for the New York State teaching certificate—we simply did the arithmetic. The B.A. degree in New York State is normally awarded for the accumulation of 120 credits. Our students spent four years at the college in taking the B.A. degree, with three courses (or actually three areas of study) each year. This would be the equivalent of thirty credits a year in the conventional system, or ten credits for a course.

We therefore dutifully awarded ten credit units in the area required for certification and made sure that the students receiving the credit possessed a rich body of knowledge and a demonstrated competence in the certified area. We did so in a variety of ways, mainly by reports from the students themselves, work sheets they kept, comments from their teachers, and sometimes statements from their employers or supervisors in agencies, schools, or organizations. Antioch College has a much more elaborate system of placement and assessment in work-study programs and has gone further than most other colleges in uniting work and study in every part of the curriculum.

When Sarah Lawrence organized its Center for Continuing Education in the late 1950s and early 1960s, it was a simple matter to transfer this way of dealing with students to the special problem of the returning student who had left college before finishing the degree. The crucial point in the work of the center was the assessment of what the returning student had done in high school, college, and the intervening years. Until that had been discussed, studied, and some plans made for the next stage in the student's education, little of worth could be decided about what the future course of study should be. Returning students needed more than anything else to consider what to do with their lives, how best to use their talents, and then to consider what sort of educational plans made the most sense in reaching the goals they had set for themselves.

We come here to another of the submerged facts in American higher education. The person who seeks an education, whether by returning to college in later years or in the first year after high school or at any other point, must involve himself in discovering the meaning of his own life and the relation between who he is and what he might become. Without that vision of a personal future and a hard look at the reality of one's own situation, the ultimate purpose of education itself—that is, to grow, to change, to liberate oneself—is almost impossible to achieve.

The college at its best is an instrument through which the individual can make such discoveries and act upon them. It is an instrument of transition from one stage in life to the next, a time for deepening and broadening the range of human experience. That range has intellectual, emotional, social, cultural, and political dimensions, and the college must organize itself in such a way that it not only makes such experience possible for the individual, but insists upon it as a responsibility both for the institution and for the person who enters it. True education begins with the enlargement of consciousness.

At a time when there are so many human problems and so few places to take them, this function of the college becomes more and more important to its service as a social institution. We have seen a series of liberation movements emerge from the 1960s into the 1970s and the development of a wider consciousness than we have ever had in our society of the possibilities and necessities of life. These movements have social and historical roots, but they emerge primarily through the growth of awareness in every sector of the population that the society and the life we lead in it are far more constricted than we formerly realized and that the constrictions are both antihuman and unnecessary. At the same time, it is now clear that the constrictions can be changed if the proper strategies are found and applied.

The development of a sense of identity within the black community, among the American Indians and the Spanish-speaking minority, among women, among young people is the forerunner of social and political action to change the rules of the society. Among the first rules to be changed are those of the educational system, whose policies have excluded minorities and lower-income groups from admission to colleges and universities. That exclusion begins in lack of access to education of sufficient quality in the earlier stages to make it possible to qualify for admission to the later stages.

But it is not only within the repressed minorities that the pressure for change has been generated. Men and women of all ages and conditions are reconsidering the lives they are leading. Many of those who have been settled in their ways, who have not thought in former years of changing or growing, now see that through the renewal of their education something new and liberating can happen to their lives. There are at least eighty million Americans between the ages of sixteen and sixty who are interested in going on with their education, and approximately thirty million others are already involved in one or another form of self-improvement through educational programs.

This has meant that over the past ten years thousands of people who have never been to college or who have dropped out at various stages are applying for admission. As Peter Meyer points out, they bring with them an assortment of qualifications which include practical experience in the vocational, technical, and professional sectors of society, along with traditional academic certificates. The question of how to assess in educational terms the life experience of these thousands of new applicants raises the deeper question which Mr. Meyer has done his best to answer: What constitutes certifiable knowledge in the culture of the four-year college or the graduate school? It would be foolish to ignore the difference in preparation for college between an eighteen-year-old whose total experience has consisted in attending school and watching television for twelve years and the police officer Mr. Meyer cites who has had a successful career at the interface of criminal justice and the problems of contemporary society. The police officer does not belong in an introductory sociology course. His direct experience with the sociology of contemporary America is an important means of understanding the principles of social action. The estimate of what he has learned cannot be based simply on the number of years he has spent in the police force. It is perfectly possible to have served in that capacity without learning anything at all about the science of society. What we need is a whole new way of considering admission to college and of developing plans for adapting the college curriculum to student needs. The two processes go together. The college must take full account of who its students are, what they bring with them from their past lives, and how they can best be given the education they need to go forward from where they are.

One of the best examples of imaginative planning of this kind is to be found in the work of the College for Human Services in New York City. The college was founded in 1964 "to train women from low-income neighborhoods in New York City for community service" and has gone on from there to develop a two-year professional curriculum in collaboration with community agencies in the city. The criteria for admission are not based on formal academic credentials, but on "demonstrated interest and aptitude for performance as professionals in the human services." The curriculum is planned with the cooperation of the student, the counseling staff, the faculty of the college, and the community agencies, and incorporates "education for work as part of education for life. . . . The content and purpose of the liberal arts . . . will be interwoven with professional education." In the past, the college has awarded the Associate in Arts degree for two years of work-study and has now applied for permission to grant a professional degree.

One of the most important contributions made by Mr. Meyer's book to educational reform in this direction lies in the illustrations it gives of how such a new system of admissions and individual planning can be organized. If the applicant has served for two years in the Peace Corps or VISTA, has been a medical technician, or has held a variety of jobs in the human services, the first step of a college must be to ask him to prepare an account of what he has learned from his experiences, in order to decide at what point in the curriculum of the college he should begin his work. This assignment is the first stage in his continuing education. Not only does it present his credentials for admission and the award of academic credit, but it gives him the opportunity to review his past experience and to say something specific about what it means to him and what he has learned from it. Whether or not he goes on to college, the review, and his own analysis of what he has gone through, is an important way of raising his own level of consciousness.

I would like to see this kind of evaluation made by every applicant to college, of whatever age and of whatever personal history. The reader will find in *Awarding College Credit for Non-College Learning* some of the forms and documents used by colleges in assessing an applicant's qualifications for academic credit. The reader will also find descriptions of seminars and discussion groups in which applicants for credit can work together in analyzing and evaluating the learning gained from their previous experience.

How useful it would be if all students, high school graduates or anyone else, could in their first year of college work with others to find ways of expressing what they have already learned through past experience and how useful or useless it has been to their total education. Once it is granted that education is a great deal more than study within the academic disciplines and that many people who have done badly in high school are quite intelligent and are in many ways equipped for further study, the task becomes one not of excluding them from admission by their lack of credentials but of measuring their readiness and of making a curriculum related to their talents and capacities.

There is much to be learned on this point from the lessons of the Chinese cultural revolution. The Chinese had been saddled with a system of higher education which had little relevance to the problems of contemporary China. The bureaucracy of the academies had made the universities into a separate body of scholars and students who controlled the cultural and intellectual life of the country. Peasants and workers were excluded from admission by the demands the universities made for proper academic credentials. The critical point in the revolution was the overthrow of the idea that higher education is a matter only of academic disciplines and the substitution of the idea that education is a mode of experience open to all.

The radical quality of the revolution is to be seen not only in the fact that the Chinese closed down the universities for four years while they reconsidered the social and cultural functions of higher education, but in the fact that learning centers for higher education have now been located in the factories and towns and not restricted to centralized university campuses. In the United States we have preserved the campus idea and are now taking preliminary steps to open up the campuses to all who wish to use them. What the Chinese did by revolution we are now trying to do by the methods of gradualism.

It turns out, after all, that as prosaic an enterprise as awarding college credit for non-college experience has within it the seeds of a radical reform in the American system of education. It forces the educator to think in new terms about the nature of humanistic learning and the goals of higher education. An avid reader with a library card and some like-minded and interested friends can reach a level of literary or social understanding beyond that of an institutionalized English major in fairly short order. Why should he not be recognized? Why should he not be included as a member of the college community among students and scholars at his own level of competence? Or, conversely, why should he be forced to take his place at a given point in the academic hierarchy only because he has been certified as the possessor of credits?

Mr. Meyer's book helps to answer these questions by giving a prescription for an alternate educational system. It is a system that is harder to operate than the conventional one. It takes a great deal more time and energy to make an individual assessment of the quality of a student's learning than it does to record his grades and credits in the registrar's office. It also takes a high degree of involvement by teachers in planning individual curricula, in counseling, in organizing seminars, and in developing new kinds of materials for use by the students.

But in the long run Mr. Meyer's prescription marks the direction educational reform must take if the American college is to serve the needs of the people and deal with a new population of students, from the younger and the older generation, from the culture of the poor, the workers, and the minorities. As an educationally underdeveloped country the United States has the same problem as other underdeveloped countries. The problem is how to develop to the full the human resources which exist in such abundance and how to arrange an educational system which values the citizen for his talents and his capacities and not for the certificates hanging on his wall.

New York

HAROLD TAYLOR

꒰꒰꒰꒱꒱꒱

Preface

In the fall of 1963 thirty eager students began their studies in a special program for adults at Queens College, City University of New York (CUNY). Those of us who initiated the Adult Collegiate Education (A.C.E.) program believed that students returning to college after anywhere from five to twenty-five years should be given formal recognition for what they had learned in the interim through their life and work experiences. Although the A.C.E. program was modeled after the special degree program for adults at Brooklyn College, we had few and sketchy guidelines for granting such credit. The Educational

Testing Service had introduced its College Level Examination Program (CLEP), and Queens was one of the first institutions to use it—but at first only as part of the screening mechanism for admission to the A.C.E. program. Not until some years later did we at Queens use the CLEP exams to grant credit at the freshman and sophomore level.

Instead, we devised a mechanism which involved the regular faculty of the college in assessing the nonacademic learning of prospective students who claimed knowledge equivalent to that covered in courses then offered at Queens. We begged, persuaded, and cajoled a small group of faculty to believe that it is possible to examine what a student knows regardless of the source of that knowledge—for example, that a person who has operated a nursery school for thirteen years, who has supervised student teachers, and who has written three textbooks in early childhood education can be given credit for knowing the methods of early childhood education.

To these first students of the A.C.E. program I fondly dedicate this book. Had it not been for their courage, tenacity, and wisdom, all the abstract arguments about the merit of crediting prior learning would have been for nought. But because of their ability, eventually every academic department at Queens was participating in awarding course credit to A.C.E. students.

The number of colleges and universities now involved in the process of crediting prior learning exceeds one hundred. They are found in every geographic region and in both the public and private sectors of higher education; among them are small as well as large institutions—traditional as well as experimental—special programs operating within larger institutions, and institutions totally dedicated to making the crediting of prior learning an integral part of every student's program.

The literature, unfortunately, does not reflect this growth. While the past five years have seen an explosion of publications on nontraditional study, the entire area of crediting prior nonacademic learning has been sadly neglected. Test-based models of crediting through CLEP and other standardized examinations have received some attention, but faculty-based models have received almost none. In 1971, when a dean of one of the first statewide external degree programs in the nation asked me where he could find written guidelines for crediting life/work experiences, I had to admit that they were in the heads of about eight people scattered throughout the country. Even now there is a paucity of written material.

Most of us who have been directly involved in the process have been "too busy" to sit back and reflect on our activities and their implications. In the early days many of us felt that the climate was not right to present a synoptic and systematic study of crediting prior learning because of the extremely limited acceptance of the process. While acceptance today is far from universal, the climate does seem to be right, and as is evident in the ensuing chapters, the need for such a work exists.

The major purposes of the book are to demonstrate the need for establishing faculty-based models for granting academic credit for learning achieved through nonacademic life/work experiences; to explain the academic merit of the process; to examine the process as it exists in a variety of institutions, using interview transcriptions and other written data as examples; to identify some of the major problems of the process and suggest solutions; to offer specific guidelines for implementing new programs; and to offer some recommendations for further study and action.

The book is limited to the examination and crediting of *prior* learning. Although experiential education can be looked at as a continuum from prior to present to future learning events, this book does not deal with directed internships, field work, study abroad programs, or any other learning endeavor that is supervised by a faculty member. The book deals only with those learning experiences a student or potential student has before intervention by any member of the examining and credentialing institution.

The book also examines only undergraduate education, although I recognize the need to consider the burgeoning number of master's and doctoral programs granting credit for life/

work experiences. The reason for the limitation to undergraduate programs is simply that there are many more programs at this level than at the graduate level.

I focus on faculty-based models of granting credit for prior learning. Although all the programs studied grant credit for formal course work taken at other institutions and make the CLEP examinations available to students who want them, the overriding need at this moment is to improve and expand direct faculty involvement in the assessment and evaluation of prior learning.

Most importantly, this book concentrates on the process of granting credit for prior learning, illustrated with examples from a number of programs. Any directory attempting to cover all existing programs would be outdated when published since more and more institutions are initiating the practice almost daily.

The data for this book were gathered basically from three sources: my personal experience with people and programs involved in the process, interviews with students and faculty at several institutions, and replies to a letter sent to the fifty-one state governing boards (including the District of Columbia) or coordinating commissions of higher education for senior colleges and the forty-six governing boards or commissions for community colleges. (Five states do not have separate boards or commissions for community colleges.) This letter stated the purpose of the study and asked for the names of programs and people involved in crediting prior learning. The number of replies to this initial letter was amazing. The senior college response was forty-two, or 82 percent, and the community college response was twenty-five, or 54 percent. These high percentages, coupled with the strongly positive quality of the remarks, are certainly one indication of national interest in the process. All programs and people cited in these letters were sent a request for information regarding their crediting methods. Only about 6 percent of the programs contacted did not reply at all. The 94 percent who wrote me were all eager to be helpful, and, from this group as well as from personal contacts, I selected the institutions I would visit and those from which I would gather only written material.

The complete list of institutions which had developed written guidelines on policy and procedures appears at the end of the book. Institutions and programs which indicated they were involved but had no written guidelines, as yet, are not included. The institutions listed are not the only ones involved in the process however. For example, all the University Without Walls (UWW) programs of the Union for Experimenting Colleges have some faculty-based method of granting credit for prior learning. I included only two of these programs because I thought these two were representative.

The fourteen institutions I chose for visits were a cross-section of public and private, small and large. I also made some attempt at geographical representation. At each institution I employed an interview schedule to gather factual data as well as to ascertain attitudes and opinions. At five of the fourteen, I interviewed only faculty and administrators; in the remaining nine I also interviewed students. I held formal interviews with two other directors of programs and with two people unaffiliated with specific institutions but vitally interested in the process. All in all, I taped interviews with twenty-one administrators and counselors, twenty-one students, and twenty faculty members, and made contact with many people throughout the country. Rather than being presented in a rigid statistical manner, the data gathered are used freely throughout the book to illustrate various aspects of the need, rationale, process, problems, and recommendations because the topic lends itself best to analysis by example.

Acknowledgments

The research for this book was made possible through a generous individual grant from the Ford Foundation. I am deeply grateful to the Foundation and especially to Gail Spangenberg, who had faith in the subject matter and in my ability to carry out the task.

The students, faculty, and administrators of the institutions I visited gave most generously of their time and talents. The hundreds of people with whom I have corresponded were also very generous and have made me feel that I am not alone in being somewhat confused but terribly optimistic about the future of crediting prior learning.

Most special thanks and sincere appreciation are due Joseph Mulholland, with whom I have had an ongoing dialogue for the past eleven years, who worked with me at Queens, and who has since built another successful program at Fordham University. He read the first draft and made many helpful suggestions. Jules Pagano, whose insights into the entire area of adult education and external degrees have been generously shared with me, also deserves a note of special gratitude. Dabney Park, Jr., has given much time to help me think through the rather complex issues at hand. He also read the first draft and his critique was extremely useful. Cyril Houle and Jonathan Warren read the first draft too; my thanks to them for their most constructive criticism.

Allan Tucker of the Florida Board of Regents has been helpful in sharing with me his special insights into nontraditional and traditional education. Jane Lichtman of Nexus at the American Association for Higher Education has been a constant gadfly and has forced me to look at all aspects of the process. Jerry Miller of the American Council on Education (Office on Educational Credit) has been of great assistance in sharing ideas and materials, as has Leland Medsker of the Center for Research and Development in Higher Education at Berkeley. Thanks are also due John Valley, of Educational Testing Service, who has shared much material and sources of new material with me. Grover Andrews of the Southern Association of Colleges and Schools also has helped by sharing most generously of his time and knowledge. Special thanks are due Adele Edwards and Patricia Shuler, who transcribed nearly sixty hours of taped interviews.

Finally, without the help, encouragement, patience, and counseling and interviewing skills of my research assistant, Mary Meyer, this work would still be at its beginning. She has helped with all aspects, from exchanging ideas to typing to holding interviews at many of the institutions visited to endless hours of encouragement.

Miami   PETER MEYER
January 1975

༉༉༉ፈፈፈ

Contents

Awarding College Credit for Non-College Learning

⫷⫸⫷⫸⫷⫸

A Guide to Current Practices

Chapter I

ᴂᴂᴂᴕᴕᴕ

Need and Academic Rationale

Pressing philosophical and practical reasons require American colleges and universities to become involved with the process of crediting prior learning, that is, those *nonacademic* life or work experiences which students have acquired before formal contact with the institution and for which they desire recognition in the form of credits toward degrees. Institutions vary in their own labels for this process: Central Michigan University credits "developmental experience," Goddard College refers to "critical life experiences," Pace University uses "life experience equivalency," Evergreen State College grants "external credit," while The College of New Rochelle awards "life experience credits." Some of these designations are misleading because they do not reflect accurately what is being credited, and because almost all programs grant credit for what has been learned rather than for the experience itself. *Prior learning* is used as the generic term throughout this book.

Regardless of labels, many institutions are already involved in the process, and even more seek assistance in trying it. Their need to grant credit for prior learning is inexorably linked with the need for educational programs and institutions which respond to changes in student population and educational methodology. In recent years these changes have stimulated the nontraditional study and innovative education movements, and crediting prior learning has been identified as one of their major components. Thus, while Rodney Hartnett of Educational Testing Service recognizes that the means for assessing nonacademic learning are not easily developed and that "nontraditional study should not be regarded as a means of getting credit for having lived a 'well-rounded' life," he agrees that it should be "a flexible program of granting recognition for academic accomplishments" (Gould and Cross, 1972, p. 22). Patricia Cross and John Valley observe that, "not surprisingly, granting credit has become a central issue in the nontraditional movement" (Cross, Valley, & Associates, 1974, p. 6). It is also one of the most problematic. In a national survey of 1,184 institutions for the Commission on Non-Traditional Study, Ruyle and Geiselman found that out of seventeen problems that have confronted institutions developing nontraditional programs, "the two most commonly reported are lack of funds and difficulty in assessing nonclassroom learning" (Cross, Valley, and Associates, 1974, p. 87).

Wherever the process is adopted it should be seen as an integral part of the program of the institution. Therefore, any discussion of the need for crediting prior learning must take into account all the needs of students that the institution is attempting to meet. Every aspect of students' education is important. While prior learning is the major focus of this book, its setting in a total educational context must be recognized.

The crediting of prior learning should not be misinterpreted as an isolated part of the total process of learning and credentialing.

The bulk of the material for this book, which offers a synoptic treatment of crediting prior learning, was gathered by mail; through personal interviews with faculty, students, and administrators at fourteen institutions throughout the country; and through interviews with educators affiliated with national education and accrediting associations. The quotes of students and educators used throughout the book come from taped interviews unless otherwise noted.

Our Credentialing Society

In one sentence Harold Hodgkinson sums up where the higher education community finds itself in relation to credentialing: "Access to the *credentialing* process is still contingent to a large extent on the amount of higher education, or its equivalent, that one has been exposed to" (Hodgkinson, 1974, p. 1). The fact that we are a credentialing society is undeniable. Although some credentials may be earned outside academe, the higher status, better paying, and most sought after positions use the college education and its credential, the degree, to certify who may be admitted to them.

The use of the academic degree as a door to employment benefits is criticized in at least two quarters. Some educators continue to argue that the degree was never meant to be work oriented; it should be the mark of the educated person. As they see it, the intrinsic value of a college education lies in its production of well-rounded, free-thinking, responsible, and cultured citizens. Other critics find the academic credit absurd (Taylor, 1971), believing that demonstrated competences and accomplishments are better qualifications for advanced education as well as employment. Both these views have merit, of course, but neither negates the fact that the academic degree is still much in demand by all segments of society.

Like it or not, we are a credentialing society. So long as the *academic* credential, specifically, provides such varied economic and social gains—and therefore many people are locked out of the reward system because they lack the credential, not because they lack the knowledge or skill or competence required—there will continue to be many who seek this diploma.

The necessity of credentialing for the public good (Miller, 1973) is not at issue here. Society has always exercised its right to protect its members from harm by licensing, credentialing, certifying, and any combination of these. Most would agree that "third-party validation of qualified individuals is essential to the orderly functioning of our society and, in many cases, for the protection of the health and safety of the public" (Hynes, 1973, p. 4). What is at issue is the fact that since the academic degree is still a credential desired by those whom it will benefit, the higher education community has a responsibility to make it available to all who can qualify.

Much attention has been paid to the notion of equal access to postsecondary education in the past ten years. For the most part, the higher education community has responded by changing admission standards, increasing the network of community colleges and other postsecondary options, and offering a variety of curricula to meet ever-changing needs. Such nontraditional postsecondary offerings as the external degree, time-liberated curricula, and off-campus educational opportunities are in the forefront of attempts to provide equal access for all.

However, nearly all of the thrust toward equality has been aimed at *future* learning possibilities. Little attention has been directed to increasing access to the academic credentialing mechanism through *prior* learning. While a tremendous effort has been launched to open the doors of the university to the formerly excluded, namely, minorities, women, and adult students, little recognition has been given to all the learning that persons possess as they walk through the door. The American Council on Education's Commission on Accreditation of Service Experiences (now the Office on Educational Credit), in arguing for expansion of its activities, put the equity of social rewards most strongly when it said, "Social justice requires that all learning, regardless of where it takes place, be treated as equitably as possible in the system of social rewards for individual knowledge and competencies. An important part of that interface is the provision of an accepted and valid system for the evaluation and recognition of learning achieved by non-traditional means" (American Council on Education, 1974, p. 11).

From Teaching to Learning

In all segments of the educational system learning is replacing teaching as the center of attention. This change in emphasis is increasing the need to assess and credit prior learning. Primary and secondary school educators as well as those engaged in higher education increasingly recognize that the focus needs to be on how, why, and what people learn, rather than on how faculty impart knowledge. This position is amply demonstrated by the many individualized learning programs available from kindergarten through postgraduate education. The focus on learning and its outcomes is also evident in the growing number of "open classrooms" in the lower grades and in the rise of competency- and/or performance-based curricula in postsecondary education. Terms such as "The Learning Society" and "lifelong learning" bespeak this changing emphasis. Nontraditional *study,* not nontraditional *teaching,* is the current headliner (although the latter still receives considerable attention).

Not only is the emphasis shifting from teaching to learning, but learning is being seen more and more as a lifetime activity. There is nothing really new in the notion that learning takes place continuously from birth to death. What is new is the concept that creditable, certifiable learning occurs throughout life and that the certifying and credentialing institutions of our society need to recognize this. "It makes little difference where or how learning takes place, whether it occurs in the classroom or on a job, at age 20 or 50 or 70, so long as it does take place, and under the circumstances appropriate to the learner. Education for adults as well as children should be centered on the needs of the learner" (The Study on Continuing Education and the Future, n.d.).

Many recent major reports dealing with the future of

higher education explore and expound this theme (Carnegie
Commission on Higher Education, 1971, 1972; Commission on
Non-Traditional Study, 1973), as do the programs and institutions discussed in this book. The faculty we interviewed stated
that they derive great satisfaction from helping students learn,
not from teaching itself.

The emphasis on learning and the learner has a clear and
direct connection with the need to grant credit for prior learning. It is impossible to know accurately where the student is
beginning unless *all* he or she has learned is assessed and evaluated. Ideally, such a process means taking into account all the
factors, formal and informal, that have contributed to the student's base of knowledge, skills, and competences.

New Position for Adult Students

Another obvious reason for crediting previous learning
is that we are serving different students. Colleges and universities are seriously courting the adult student. In part their
action is a logical outcome of accepting the philosophy of lifelong learning. A more powerful cause is the rather startling
realization that enrollment of the "normal" college age student is declining, as is the potential number of eighteen-year-
olds for the future. Faculty and administrators who have not
had the opportunity before to work with the adult student are
also encouraging institutional interest. This new acceptance of
older students indicates that colleges and universities *can* adapt
to the changing needs of an increasingly complex society.

Adult students have been seen on campuses for many
years, of course. In the past, however, both the adult students
and those concerned with them were relegated to second-class
citizenship. In an address I delivered nearly ten years ago to a
group of adult evening students (I was then an administrator in
an evening program) I described the attitudes encountered.
"Many of my colleagues are convinced that there is something
drastically wrong with me because I have elected to devote my
energies to what they consider to be a suspect area of higher
education. Just as the evening student is often seen as some-

thing less than the day student, so the evening faculty member or administrator is sometimes seen as not quite up to his day-session counterpart. After all, if you were really on the ball, you would be concerning yourself with the essence of the university —educating full-time day session students" (Meyer, 1965). At that time of great upheaval and student unrest, faculty were retreating to contemplate their own fates as well as that of the universities, and the adult student was being neglected because of these other pressures.

As the turmoil of the 1960s gave way to the 1970s the climate for dealing seriously with the adult student improved considerably. Perhaps as a reaction to the radical student movements of the 1960s—which, after all, were staffed primarily by younger students—the adult emerged as the seriously motivated student. Whatever the reason, many institutions today are committed to the adult student as their primary focus rather than as a secondary byproduct.

For example, Florida International University, a new state institution which opened its doors to more than five thousand students in September 1972, has a student population whose mean age is 27. Courses are offered from 8:00 a.m. until 11:00 p.m. and 60 percent of the students register for courses that begin at 6:00 p.m. or later. The same faculty serves the entire student body. No distinction is made in course prefixes, such as "E" for evening. The same curriculum and services are available to all students. The division of continuing education is strictly an administrative function without a faculty or a curriculum. The FIU model is not uncommon today, but it is an innovation in light of what was prevalent ten to fifteen years ago.

Another example of the coming of age of the adult student is the fact that the Association of University Evening Colleges has changed its name to the Association for Continuing Higher Education, thus recognizing that evening colleges, as such, are more than likely on their way out and that the concept of lifelong learning is here to stay.

Nontraditional programs which originated in the vacuum left by the 1960s are primarily geared to the self-sufficient, self-reliant adult students. Faculty and administrators agree that the students they assess and evaluate for credit for prior learning are exceptional insofar as they *are* more adult, more mature, and more seriously motivated than most of the regular younger students; as they see it, it makes more sense to grant credit for prior learning to the adult student than to the younger student, in that the longer one lives, the more experiences there are from which to learn.

We have only begun to deal with the tip of the iceberg. There are many more potential adult students with creditable prior learning than there are programs to serve them. Most administrators of these programs report that they have never had to advertise formally. Word of mouth carried the message into the community and many programs have to maintain waiting lists because their resources cannot handle large numbers of students.

If the focus on lifelong learning continues, postsecondary institutions, especially colleges and universities, will need to make some fundamental changes if they are going to respond to the challenge (Carnegie Commission on Higher Education, 1971). The emergence of the adult student who is engaged in continuing education presents a great opportunity for renewal. The despair being felt by those who are acutely aware of declining enrollments can be turned into genuine hope because, "while some *traditional* 'doors of education' are now closing, some *nontraditional* ones are beginning to swing open. As Dickens said, 'the worst of times' can also be 'the best of times' depending on our point of view, and there is some reason to believe that higher education may be entering a period of great renaissance, rather than decline" (Boyer, 1974, p. 2). As an example of the pool to draw upon, Boyer points out that the number of adults engaged in some form of full-time college study tripled between 1960 and 1970 from 9.6 million to 25 million. An estimated 80 million older persons will participate in some form of education in 1974–1975. Not all of these will be in colleges but all will be receiving some form of education.

Increasing the adult student population in institutions of higher education, or responding to the buyer's market, as some put it, increases the need for crediting prior learning. If we are to continue the move toward making learners central to the educational process, then those learners, adults with a variety of learning experiences already behind them, have the right to have that learning assessed and evaluated for academic credit. To do less would be to perpetuate a system of social injustice. The students will not allow that to happen. The institutions of higher education cannot allow the injustice to continue.

National Trends

A number of important educational groups are making recommendations or undertaking studies which reflect the need to credit prior learning and the need for some guidance in making this process an integral part of educational programs.

The American Council on Education's Office on Educational Credit plans as one of its three major new functions to recommend "to colleges and universities policies and procedures for the measurement and awarding of educational credit for nonformal learning experiences" (American Council on Education, 1974, p. 22).

The Commission on Colleges of the Southern Association of Colleges and Schools (SACS) has established a Committee on Non-Traditional Considerations whose purpose is to review all standards and procedures of accreditation so that guidelines can be established for awarding credit for prior learning as well as for other nontraditional efforts. A similar committee has been established at the Western Association of Schools and Colleges (WASC). Both accrediting associations are concerned that crediting prior learning be grounded in sound academic policies and practices.

At least two national studies presently under way deal, at least in part, with crediting prior learning. The Center for Research and Development in Higher Education at the University of California, Berkeley, is assessing new institutional forms for extending postsecondary education: (1) external study of traditional degree curricula, (2) new curricula and degrees to extend postsecondary education, (3) new time dimensions for learning, and (4) forms that provide extensive credit for previous achievement and experience. The outcomes of each program will be evaluated in terms of how well they are meeting the objectives set by the institution when the program was initiated, and the overall educational and social consequences of each of the four nontraditional forms will also be assessed. The interdisciplinary team engaging in this study is directed by Leland Medsker and is being funded by the National Science Foundation.

The Cooperative Assessment of Experiential Learning (CAEL) is a Carnegie Corporation–funded project of The Educational Testing Service (ETS) whose overall objective is to "bring about a more rational integration of formal schooling and practical experience, partly by recognizing accomplishment wherever it occurs and also by systematically including experiential learning in the curriculum" (Educational Testing Service, 1973, p. 1). Nine institutions compose the cooperative national consortium that provides both the steering (policy) committee and the working committee of the project. All nine are involved with at least one form of experiential education, be it the assessment of prior learning or the structuring of future learning events. Other institutions interested in experiential education have been invited to form a CAEL Assembly which will serve as a forum for discussion of problems of mutual concern. The Assembly is to meet two or three times per year; membership is open to any recognized degree-granting institution actively engaged in experiential education and interested in participating in CAEL activities, such as trying out new materials to be developed by the project.

In the Preface I mentioned that almost all (82 percent) of the Statewide Boards of Regents or Coordinating Commissions for Higher Education responded positively to our initial request for information on their efforts. This response, plus the fact that at least six states (Connecticut, Illinois, Michigan, Pennsylvania, Washington, and Wisconsin) currently have detailed plans for establishing statewide external degree programs or open universities, is further indication of the national interest in crediting prior learning. These six, of course, are in addition to those states such as Florida and New York which are already operating statewide external degree programs.

As these and other national trends become more visible and as more and more potential students learn of the alternative ways to receive a college education, the need for crediting prior learning will continue to increase. As it grows, so does the need for establishing sound procedures based on a solid academic rationale for carrying out the process.

Rationale

The rationale for granting credit for prior learning is actually quite simple. When we hold the learner to be the central figure in the educational process, *knowledge is valid regardless of source*. Most of the faculty-based programs which credit prior learning offer the following as a nearly self-evident truth: *all experiences* which reflect collegiate-level learning should be credited. The ABLE Program of the College of Arts and Sciences at Adelphi University states, for example: "The typical ABLE student . . . enters the program with skills and accomplishments based on years of experience. (The average age of the ABLE student is 42.) It seems appropriate that methods be developed to officially recognize those competencies which relate to academic knowledge."

The California State College at Dominguez Hills puts it this way, "Under special circumstances students may petition the Experiential Education Committee to receive credit for academically valid past experiences not reflected on any official transcript. This policy acknowledges the validity of many past activities and work experiences found particularly in the background of older students."

The University Without Walls (UWW) unit of the University of Massachusetts (Amherst) says, "For most of the individuals attracted to the University Without Walls and parallel programs at many other colleges and universities, what they learn in college is intimately related to what they learned from their personal experiences on their jobs and their roles in the community. There is a need to identify and assess the knowledge, competencies, and skills these individuals bring to college. The educational value of learning based on experiences other than those taking place in an academic setting should be recognized and validated. Past learning from experience should be used to plan and integrate present learning in college. In this way, education in college becomes an integral part of a lifelong learning experience."

The University of Wisconsin at Green Bay states the rationale as follows: "Persons not enrolled in colleges and universities frequently have many opportunities for learning. Often, the stimulus for or source of their learning stems from their involvement in activities which are similar to those experienced by UWGB students who are engaged in off-campus study or projects. It seems logical, then, that learning experiences, which persons outside of UWGB have and which are similar or equivalent to those of UWGB students, should have the potential for providing an equal number of credits. Of utmost importance is that learning has occurred."

What underlies all of these statements is a sense that crediting prior learning is worth doing, almost unquestionably and self-evidently to those who have studied the issues. The process of granting credit for prior learning is clearly one of assessing and evaluating an individual's experiences or knowledge by one or more faculty members who have a set of standards against which to measure experiences and a set of tools available to accomplish this end. That a particular set of standards may be vague or ill-defined should not cloud the fact that knowledge, skills, and competences appropriate to college-level work can be evaluated. Although some of the tools used are roughly hewn, we can still perceive that an examination process is under way. Once so understood, much of the mystery disappears and crediting prior learning is recognized as a natural part of a total learning program. Combining faculty-based assessment with credit for standardized examinations allows students and faculty to plan the kind of future learning events that make maximum use of what has already been learned.

This process places control over the curriculum squarely

in the hands of individual faculty members and students. Many professors and students involved in crediting prior learning report a rapport with each other *and with the curriculum* never felt before. A true partnership in learning was achieved in many instances because of the rich backgrounds of the students and the faculty members' willingness to share in that background for their own growth. One teacher's greatest satisfaction with the process was "dealing with a student who has practical experience which complements my theoretical or book experience in terms of a learning process for me." Those faculty who in recent years have felt removed from some of the basic considerations of curriculum can rest assured that granting credit for prior learning will allow them as deep an involvement as they wish. For this undertaking requires us to ask: Exactly what will be credited? How much credit shall be awarded for what kinds of learning? Does prior learning have to be tied to future educational goals? It is impossible to answer these questions seriously without involvement in fundamental issues of curriculum.

As I mentioned earlier, the innovations of nontraditional study depend heavily on crediting prior learning. Lifelong learning and the time-liberated degree (*time-liberated* more accurately expresses the sense of the Carnegie Commission's *Less Time, More Options* than does *time-shortened*) are interrelated concepts which assume the learner to be central. Both hold that knowledge is valid regardless of source, and both call for interweaving the world of work with the world of school to accomplish a truly integrated living learning society. As the Carnegie Commission puts it:

> Society would gain if work and study were mixed throughout a lifetime, thus reducing the sense of sharply compartmentalized roles of isolated student v. workers and of youth v. isolated age. The sense of isolation would be reduced if more students were also workers and if more workers could also be students; if the ages mixed on the job and in the classroom in a more normally structured type of community; if all members of the community valued both study and work and had a better chance to understand

the flow of life from youth to age. Society would be more integrated across the lines that now separate students and workers, youth and age [1971, p. 2].

In the ultimate living-learning society there would be no need to credit prior learning, for all learning would be equally rewarded. However, until that ultimate is reached, crediting previous educational experiences is an essential part of the life of students.

While the rationale for granting credit for prior learning is simple, it raises once again some much tougher questions: What constitutes the baccalaureate degree and who determines who is educated? As the nontraditional study movement considers new forms, processes, time-frames, and locations of teaching and learning, we are forced to reexamine our underlying goals. Samuel Gould states the situation well:

> We are all so much involved in the impedimenta of learning—the access, the measuring, the grading, the institutional structures, the financing, the governance, the bricks and mortar, the degree-granting process—that we forget the basic issue. . . . What is it all intended to achieve? What are the characteristics of an educated person, and what can a college or university or any agency or any experience contribute toward creating such a person? . . . What are the desirable outcomes of *any* degree to be acquired by the student? These questions are actually more fundamental than those that preoccupy the proponents of change. The answers to them are still vague in contrast to the detailed mechanics of new programs being fashioned. Every institution and every educator will have to wrestle with such questions and answers if more than superficial solutions are to be reached [Vermilye, 1972, p. 183].

Many faculty members state that their struggles to assess and evaluate the knowledge, skills, and competences that students bring to the formal learning situation make them rethink the way they examine and test students in the *regular* curriculum. This reappraisal, in turn, leads them to look at curriculum content and then to question the purpose of education or the degree.

Clearly, the rationale for crediting prior learning may be associated with some disturbing self-examination. The more open-ended the process is, the more anxieties it raises about the fundamental values of the entire educational enterprise. Many faculty are reluctant to become involved for this reason. This is why tried and true mechanisms such as the transfer of credits from another accredited institution and standardized examinations are preferred over those mechanisms which directly involve faculty in evaluation and assessment. This is why almost all faculty say there should be institutional, regional, or national guidelines for the process but are reluctant to specify them because of the individuality and uniqueness of each students' set of prior learning experiences. These anxieties and concerns are not easily dealt with, yet we must be aware of their impact on implementing the crediting process.

Common Resistances

In addition to the general fears I just described, I frequently encounter a number of more specific reasons for not becoming involved in granting credit for prior learning. The first of these is seldom spoken aloud but underlies all the others. The gist of it is that "if you haven't learned it from me in my classroom, you haven't learned it." It would be a grave error to dismiss this statement lightly, especially when "it" refers to a set of values rather than pure knowledge. While this attitude is perhaps more prevalent among the professions, humanities, and social sciences than in the natural sciences, it is evident in all disciplines. Every group of faculty has defined a curriculum that it defines as its version of the truth.

Faculty members must be willing to admit that their curriculum is value-laden and *should* be willing to acknowledge that students can demonstrate competences which are acceptable but reflect a different value system. This decision rests with the faculty-student body at each institution. Once made, the resistance to prior learning can at least be dealt with in an open, honest manner.

Another argument holds that the process is too subjective. However, once it is seen as an examination procedure not unlike so many others to which students are subjected, some of the resistance begins to ebb. Furthermore, when one points out the presence of subjectivity in assessing learning in on-campus courses, more resistance recedes. There does not seem to be any need to apologize for a certain amount of subjectivity in judging on-campus or off-campus learning. Human frailty has been tolerated for centuries and no one claims infallibility when it comes to conducting examinations. What *is* curious and somewhat questionable is that many faculty envision much more stringent measures for off-campus or experiential education than they utilize for on-campus evaluation. And when faculty move from dealing with off-campus education to crediting prior learning, even more stringency is evidenced.

One student mentioned in an interview for this study that the paper she prepared for documenting prior learning was worth "three As in my hardest courses," according to one of her instructors. Most portfolios and their documentation require more student effort than would normally be required in a course or courses bearing the same number of credits.

A third source of resistance is that faculty do not like to view themselves as credentialers or certifiers, as they feel threatened in this role. As Mulholland (1973, p. 5) expresses it, "If . . . students can obtain through their experience what university faculties have labored for and prepared to give for the greater part of their working life, then what exactly would be the justification of having faculty?" This statement might seem to present an extreme position but, extreme or not, it quite accurately reflects some deep feelings. For some reason, faculty take an either/or stance on this point. "Either I am a credentialer or I am a teacher." In reality, of course, most faculty are both, since they do certify in some manner that a student has earned credit for an event. Elbow would like to see faculty get out of the certifying business altogether. He sees a competency-based university of tomorrow that will say to a student, "We will award you the bachelor degree when you attain (a) expertise in one area, (b) some competence in three others, and (c) a basic writing skill. If you already have these attainments, you may have the degree right now. If you don't, you may get them however you please. (If you want to know precisely what we require, you may look at our file of completed exams, projects, and theses to see which ones were judged successful.) We also offer the following teaching and learning procedures which you may find helpful" (Elbow, 1971, p. 241). He believes teaching would benefit if it were removed from certifying because the dual role of ally and adversary would be removed. Perhaps so, but a teacher can never escape the fact that he or she must make judgments. Even in the role of facilitator, some judgment is necessary. Besides, the educative process demands a reciprocity of ideas and judgments. And the crediting of prior learning allows more faculty-student interchange than does the normal classroom situation.

Fourth, faculty and administrators frequently assert that the accrediting associations will not allow them to grant credit for prior learning. This charge is levelled against both regional and national accrediting bodies. While certain regional associations are slower than others in formally recognizing the many aspects of nontraditional study, there is no evidence that any specifically prohibits the crediting of prior learning. All have indicated that one of their primary objectives is to encourage experimental approaches to instruction and learning (Miller, 1973). At least two, the Southern Association of Colleges and Schools (SACS) and the Western Association of Schools and Colleges (WASC), are working on guidelines for crediting prior learning. The Federation of Regional Accrediting Commissions of Higher Education (FRACHE) has issued an interim statement on accreditation and nontraditional study. Although these guidelines are somewhat vague, they are the first national statements on the subject. Two of the general policies are: "(1) Accreditation will be considered only when a number of individuals have been granted or have qualified for a degree by various non-traditional patterns indicated. Consideration of students' completed programs and student reaction are deemed indispensable to accreditation. (2) Accreditation procedures should be comprehensive, flexible, and fair. Evaluation committees should include persons who have experience in non-traditional programs and/or are sufficiently conversant and understanding to review innovations competently" (FRACHE, 1973, p. 1).

Speaking specifically to what is and is not allowed, Andrews of SACS stated in our interview that "I think we (SACS) are used a great deal . . . as someone to hide behind. This comes from two positions: (1) they are really copping out on their institutional responsibilities to be responsive . . . and so they say that the accrediting association won't let us do that; (2) they are not aware of the changes that come about in accrediting standards and in the encouragement that the accrediting association is trying to give institutions to try to develop innovative programs."

The other accrediting bodies "hidden behind" are the national professional accrediting associations. The most frequently mentioned public certifying body is the individual state department of education. Taylor (1969, p. 193) speaks to this point when he says: "The requirements for teacher certification are administered by State Departments of Education. But . . . the requirements themselves are developed and formulated mostly by deans, department chairmen, and professors of education in the colleges of education and universities, and . . . the requirements are heavily influenced by a variety of educational organizations, each with its own pressures for courses and credits in given disciplines. . . . The State Department is often in the role of referee rather than combatant; in many cases it needs protection rather than attack." Actually, then, the restrictions on crediting prior learning, if they exist, cannot be laid on the state's doorstep.

Another example from my own institution is useful. An accrediting team of the Council on Social Work Education (CSWE) mentioned during a recent visit that an undergraduate social work program at Florida International University might run into trouble for crediting prior learning. The program grants credit to students whose prior learning enables them to demonstrate competence in field work. They may receive credit for one or two required field instruction experiences. Each of these normally requires a student to spend 240 hours per quarter in supervised field instruction, for a total of 480 hours. The CSWE prescribes that all accredited undergraduate programs in social work shall include 300 hours of supervised field instruction. The visiting team mentioned that crediting prior learning would not show that a student had taken at least 300 hours, and therefore CSWE might disallow the process of crediting prior learning. Leaving aside the fact that the requirement is for 300 hours of exposure rather than attainment, the argument is fallacious because the credit for prior learning is given as *the equivalent of field instruction*. This means that the student has attained on his or her own what would normally be required of the student who spent the actual time in the field setting. It is up to the institution, not the accrediting body, to certify this equivalency. Once so certified, the accrediting body must accept it.

It is important to recognize that visiting teams of accrediting bodies are composed of peers, colleagues who face similar problems at their own schools. Equally important, institutions should challenge standards they feel are outdated or antithetical to legitimate innovations. To do less would be to shirk their proper responsibility.

Chapter II

ลลลหหห

Basic Decisions

One of the most common problems identified by the students, faculty, and administrators we interviewed is confusion about what aspect of prior learning is actually being credited. Is it the actual life/work experience? Is it knowledge gained from the experience? Is it insight into that knowledge? Is it the ability to write well? Is it the ability to organize the portfolio? For example, only three out of twenty-one students knew exactly what had been credited. The remainder, whether or not they thought they received a fair evaluation, gave some indication that they were unsure of what they had received credit for. Many faculty also freely admitted that they are not always clear about the exact level of abstraction desired to demonstrate the learning derived from experience. Some of these also had the courage to acknowledge that they experience similar confusion in their courses. One explained that he normally grades students on their ability to abstract from specific learning events, synthesize those abstractions to form the basis for new theoretical frameworks, and apply the new frameworks to further learning events. Students receive grades on a continuum according to their ability to perform these various feats of abstraction. Attempting to apply the same standard to prior learning proves extremely difficult and confusing for this particular faculty member. In the first place, he is told that a student either receives credit for prior learning or not; there is no "grading" possible. (Had he ever had experience with pass-fail in his courses? No.) Second, the learning achieved through life experience does not coincide exactly with what he usually covers; it is close—sometimes it actually surpasses the content normally covered—but not exact. Third, the faculty member feels quite uncomfortable because it seems as though he needs to revamp his entire assessment standards and methodology. He admits that his "normal standards" have never been clearly delineated to students at the beginning of his courses and that no one has ever asked him to do this. Probing further, we discover that students, colleagues, department chairpeople, and deans all assume that this close a scrutiny of what occurs in the classroom is not necessary and that it is an infringement of the faculty member's academic freedom. This example clearly demonstrates the need for a precise definition by the instructor of the expected outcomes of any educational event. Students have a right to know what level of abstraction is expected, what skills are to be acquired, and what content is to be learned. Such delineation also helps the instructor accurately construct what is to be learned.

What Shall Be Credited?

An analysis of the guidelines provided by the institutions and programs listed at the end of the book indicates that prior experience is being examined at at least four related, but discrete, levels. Credit may be given for: (1) the life/work experience itself; (2) the knowledge, competence, or skill gained from the experience; (3) the analysis of the learning gained from the experience; or (4) the analysis and synthesis of discrete bodies of knowledge gained from the same or different experiences.

Life/Work Experience Itself. At this first level the experience itself is considered worthy of direct translation into academic credit. The student need not demonstrate any knowledge or competence since all documentation is by third-party evaluation. The Center for Community Education of Elizabethtown College is one of the few institutions granting credit for life/work experiences per se. Their policy is described as follows:

> 1. Each year of full-time work in the area of concentration of the major chosen by the candidate will be counted as six (6) semester hours. Validation is made by an executive officer of the organization by whom the candidate is presently employed. He will sit on the Advisory-Consultative-Evaluation (ACE) Committee for the student. Other work will be validated by appropriate documents which will be considered by the ACE Committee. These will be determined for veracity from company employment records.
>
> 2. Each year of full-time work in an area other than the concentration of the major will be counted as two (2) semester hours of credit. Validation is the same as Item 1.
>
> 3. Not more than one-half the total work for a degree will be credited from work experience validation, but all work experience will be included for the record.

The *direct* translation of work experience into academic credits continues to be an issue whenever crediting prior learning is discussed. Hartnett states that "educational credentials should not be assigned to various work or travel experiences unless academically relevant outcomes of those experiences can be demonstrated" (Gould and Cross, 1972, pp. 21–22). But what are "academically relevant outcomes"? Who decides this rather crucial issue? Is what is academically relevant for one student necessarily so for another? Does the answer depend on the purposes of higher education? Is it possible to get agreement on these purposes? Is "academic relevance" defined differently by a faculty, a discipline, an institution?

There is nothing that raises a red flag faster than announcing that work experience per se will be evaluated for credit. Even the most nontraditional of the nontraditional educators is aroused on this topic. Somehow, if learning produced by the work experience is to be evaluated for credit, the red flag remains down because the core of higher education—learning—is not being challenged. And therefore almost all programs incorporate some statement that learning must have taken place before credit can be awarded. I do not favor the direct crediting of experience because, if nothing else, a collegiate education should consist of identifiable learning outcomes.

Knowledge, Competence, or Skill Gained. This is the first level of abstraction and involves direct demonstration by the student that any or all of the following have taken place: (a) knowledge has been received, as demonstrated by the student either verbally or in writing by simple listings or categorization; (b) skill or competence has been acquired and can be demonstrated by the student; (c) a product has been created, such as a piece of sculpture, a book, or a painting, which can be judged by one or more experts in the appropriate field.

Analysis of Learning Gained. This second level of abstraction deals only with the learning that has taken place. Students must demonstrate either orally or in writing an ability to analyze the learning which has taken place in relation to a larger theoretical framework.

Analysis and Synthesis of Discrete Bodies of Knowledge Gained. At the third level of abstraction, which also deals only with derived learning, students must demonstrate either orally or in writing the ability to analyze discrete bodies of knowledge gained from experience and synthesize these into one or more theoretical frameworks.

Specific examples which illustrate *each* of these levels of abstraction are difficult to find because most programs use them in combination or have not yet clarified which level they desire. Below are some examples of what is to be credited from

Brooklyn College, the University of Wisconsin at Green Bay (UWGB), The College of New Rochelle, and the California State University at San Francisco.

Brooklyn College states: "An underlying premise of the Special Baccalaureate is that the students in the program will have attained, by virtue of their work, or other sorts of non-academic learning experiences, or their own intellectual initiatives, the same degree of knowledge or competence in certain subject matter areas that younger undergraduates attain in the academic classroom."

This is an extremely clear statement which cannot be easily misinterpreted. Knowledge or competence is creditable, not the experience itself. Not all knowledge is creditable, but only that which relates directly to specific course content; and that knowledge must be the same as that expected of the regular (younger) Brooklyn College undergraduate. One infers that a faculty member could use whatever assessment procedure is being used in the classroom to judge prior learning. This interpretation is extremely narrow; its limitations make it clear to all. Not surprisingly, the more narrowly defined the concept of prior learning, the more readily understandable it is. A narrow definition uses existing procedures which have been accepted over a period of time and rests on assumptions which have long gone unquestioned. One might well ask why prior learning cannot produce knowledge *superior* to that of younger undergraduates? Is the educational standard for the degree based solely on what is prescribed for them? These are questions which rest with the faculty/student body responsible for academic policy and must be raised continually as the curriculum changes.

The University of Wisconsin at Green Bay states its policy as follows:

> From the beginning, the faculty at UWGB has recognized that there are several modes of learning. This recognition is evidenced by the fact that built into the early drafts of the Academic Plan and included in its final version were off-campus portions of the liberal education seminars,

opportunities for practica during the January Interim Period, independent study projects and communiversity projects. It has further demonstrated its commitment to off-campus learning by approving programs such as the University Year for ACTION and the University Without Walls, which significantly increased the number of degree credits that students could accumulate from off-campus learning activities and experiences. At UWGB, then, the Academic Plan is one of *applied* liberal education. Learning is not confined to the classroom.

Persons not enrolled in colleges and universities frequently have many opportunities for learning. Often, the stimulus for or source of their learning stems from their involvement in activities which are similar to those experienced by UWGB students who are engaged in off-campus study or projects. It seems logical, then, that learning experiences which persons outside of UWGB have and which are similar or equivalent to those of UWGB students should have the potential for providing an equal number of credits. Of utmost importance is that learning has occurred.

To have learning experiences evaluated for degree credit, four criteria must be satisfied. First, the student must be a registered UWGB student. Second, what was learned must be related to courses, disciplines, academic areas and/or academic programs at UWGB, if possible. Third, what was learned must be articulated. Fourth, verification and documentation of what was learned must be presented. If the learning experiences are not academically related, there is no adequate framework for evaluation. If what was learned from the experiences cannot be communicated to others, then evaluation is impossible. If evidence to verify and document the learning experiences is not presented, there is no basis for judgment and evaluation.

UWGB emphasizes learning that can be communicated in an academically acceptable manner. No specific mention is made of the level of abstraction demanded and one can only surmise that prior learning must be demonstrated at the same level of abstraction as that required for future learning.

In a document distributed to students in the New Resources Program at the College of New Rochelle, the question of what is to be credited is answered as follows: "What do we mean by life experience? Experience can be an effective teacher. What an adult learns through experience is important. What is learned through reflection on that experience is more important. Therefore, this portfolio should reflect your experience, giving a sense of what you have learned and skills you have acquired from this experience. Both are worthy of academic recognition. The most suitable form of recognition in the academic context is academic credit."

This statement, while not as specific as the one from Brooklyn College, attempts to define the desired level of abstraction. The student is told that reflection on what is experienced is more important than what has been learned. At the same time, the narrative need only contain *a sense* of what has been learned. While one infers that specifics have been delineated, careful examination forces a different conclusion. The New Resources Program does offer a "Life-experience Workshop" which teaches the student how to reflect on experience in such a way that the learning derived from it takes on an academically acceptable form.

In a similar explanatory note to students, the General Studies Division of the California State University at San Francisco explains what is creditable in the following way:

> Your task is twofold. First, document your previous experience. Second, relate the quality of your experiences as they have affected you in your personal development. The emphasis is not to be upon what you have done, but rather upon what you have learned during the process. Here are some questions that will give you a frame of reference from which to work:
> 1. How did your external learning situation expand your educational experience?
> 2. How did your external learning situation enlarge the range of applications of concepts and techniques previously acquired?
> 3. How did your external learning situation expand your intellectual, aesthetic, social, and moral viewpoints?

4. How did your external learning situation increase your understanding of the culture?

5. How did this active participation in an external learning situation allow you to realize your potentialities?

As you will note, the emphasis is not upon previous course work completed, as that was considered when you were admitted as a student. The emphasis is upon the relevance of work other than course work for which you are seeking credit.

Although the student is told that what is creditable is what has been learned rather than what has been done or experienced, the questions used as examples do not clarify what *level* of learning is desirable or acceptable. These students receive more assistance through their faculty advisors, but according to interview data, the faculty do not have any more explicit guidelines than those available to the students. Some liked this discretionary power; others would have preferred more specific guidelines.

As problematic as some of these guidelines might be, establishing a set of criteria is vital before attempts to assess prior learning begin. Not doing so causes unnecessary confusion and anxiety to faculty and students alike. One faculty member, when asked what had been his most significant problem with the process, replied: "Establishing some type of uniform practice and yet not eliminating the individuality that exists. Each person must be evaluated on his own merit and at the same time there's a need for some type of structure or uniformity. I guess this dichotomy provides me the greatest difficulty." Although some of the *process* of evaluation must emerge as it occurs, it should not be confused with what is being evaluated. The four guidelines abstracted above deal with criteria of *content*. How that content is then assessed constitutes the process of judging prior learning.

Even though all programs should have a solid grasp on what is to be credited before they begin evaluation, judgments of the creditability of events should not be made unilaterally without full discussion. The decision rests in the hands of the faculty/student body responsible for curriculum, and from the start discussion should involve the maximum number of decision makers possible. While it might be more comfortable and expeditious to include only a small group of faculty, students, and administrators who seem sympathetic and enthusiastic, it is difficult to return to the mainstream beginning with a select few. Some of the programs that began in this manner never did get wider university approval for the process. Others won grudging approval only after long, sometimes uselessly heated, debate.

The dialogue on what is creditable need not stop once the program has started. Ongoing discussion will help to ensure that the program continues to meet the changing needs of students, in relation to both future learning and prior learning. It also will help to keep the process in faculty and student hands rather than in those of the admissions personnel or registrar.

Some persons feel that once the process has proven itself and becomes generally accepted, much of the assessment can be standardized. While standardization might be desirable in some cases, the danger of forfeiting control for convenience becomes great. Also, granting credit for prior learning is in itself a learning process for faculty and students. The same limitations that currently apply to national or institutional testing programs would apply to any part of the process that became standardized.

Prior Learning and Future Goals

The question of whether or not all *creditable* prior learning must be related to the students' future educational goals is as crucial as the question of what is to be credited because it is answerable only in the context of a total educational program. Two specific examples are illustrative. One concerns an external degree program with an individualized, learner-as-central approach and the other a special program for adults with a fixed curriculum which does not consider prior learning to be an integral part of the total program. In describing how the education contract for students is devised, Florida International University states:

The first step in writing the Education Contract is to determine how much credit will be given for a student's previous academic work, creative and other life experiences and competencies. This involves determining where each student is, where his or her competencies and strengths are, and where the gaps are in terms of the educational process.

The second step is to determine what each particular student needs in order to complete the baccalaureate degree. This process involves examining each student's goals and desires and devising a strategy to match them as much as possible to the institutional and professional character of the discipline or study area which that student wishes to pursue.

This model almost always dictates that creditable learning must be related to future goals regardless of the intrinsic value of the student's knowledge. So, if a student wants a degree in political science and has extensive experience in electronic technology, the learning derived from the technology experience would probably not be credited, even though the learning derived from technology has intrinsic collegiate value. The student and advisor must make choices which, in a sense, force the future to determine the past.

Half of the fixed curriculum prescribed by the Adult Collegiate Education Program at Queens College is especially tailored to meet the needs of an adult population. The program is described as follows:

The foundation of the ACE Program is a special series of interdisciplinary seminars in the arts, sciences, and social sciences. In these small seminar groups, usually not larger than fifteen students, emphasis is placed on the intimate exchange of ideas and on intensive independent study. Successful completion of this series of seminars and a foreign-language sequence also offered by the ACE Program will constitute nearly one-half of the work for the degree. In addition, ACE provides a number of elective seminars. Most of the remaining coursework required will be in the student's major; the rest will be electives, including any life-achievement credits granted.

When a student has matriculated and completed the required 36 credits of basic ACE seminars, he may consult with an ACE counselor about his eligibility for "life-achievement" credits. A student may receive no credits, a few credits, or up to a maximum of 36, depending on his background; very few students receive the maximum of 36.

It should be clear that no student automatically qualifies for credits, but he is eligible to apply for an evaluation if his background includes achievements which, because of their resemblance to college course content, lend themselves to translation into academic credits.

The ACE Program awards life-achievement credits only after students have proven their ability to do college-level work. Crediting prior learning is seen as one alternative to completing an established set of learning events. The time spent in the program prepares students to learn how to think academically. Their processes of abstraction are sharpened and learning is rearranged so that it becomes systematic, analytical, and critical. By the time students have completed the 36 credits of ACE seminars they can reflect on their prior learning as they have been taught to do in the seminars. They are thus prepared to develop a much more academically sensitized and documented portfolio and they have gained the confidence needed to present the portfolio to the faculty for evaluation.

Whether to credit any prior learning that has academic value or to accept only that portion which applies to future goals may be a difficult decision. Only those who can handle both do not see this issue as problematic. More often than not, however, the structure of the institution and the goals of its total program force a choice. When a student presents a transcript from another institution for transfer credit, it is easier to be arbitrary about what will be accepted than it is when a student presents a vast array of documented proof that learning has taken place in a number of legitimate, but unrelated, disciplines. Many programs have not fully thought through what they are crediting and whether or not prior learning needs to be related to future goals. The students are asked to document whatever *they* think relevant to collegiate-level work with no

more guidance than that. One student arrived with two suitcases full of material and it took four faculty members six
days to wade through, sort out, and begin to make determina-
tions. Needless to say, this particular institution was ready with
extremely specific guidelines the following week.

The place of prior learning in the total program is no
less and no more important than the place of future learning
events. Programs which accept responsibility for crediting prior
learning must also grant the process and its results a proper
place in the total curriculum.

Cost

This study did not attempt a systematic cost analysis of
crediting prior learning. The data collected through interviews
and mailings did touch on cost in the following areas: source of
revenue and students' perceptions of the fairness of the cost to
them. Programs and institutions which treat the crediting of
prior learning as an integral part of the total learning program
do not, often cannot, separate the cost of crediting prior learning from the cost of the total program. In special programs
which use regular full-time faculty and counselors specifically
for crediting prior learning, it is possible to isolate the cost.
However, some of these programs also have difficulty in determining separate costs because regular faculty are used for the
entire special program, not just to assess prior learning.

The External Degree Program at Florida International
University, for example, has no faculty of its own. A professor
of English is asked to be a faculty advisor for an external degree student, for example. That professor contracts to (1) evaluate the student's prior learning, (2) help the student write the
Education Contract, (3) be available as that student's regular
advisor for the entire time it takes the student to finish the contract, and (4) supervise the student in a certain number of hours
of independent study. Students pay a $350 initial contract fee
which entitles them to all of the services listed above from the
faculty advisor plus initial counseling by a staff member of the
External Degree Program. As can be seen, it would be difficult,

though not impossible, to derive the cost of just the prior learning evaluation.

Revenue to partially or totally defray the cost of assessing prior learning comes from any or all of the following: (1) special fees paid by students, (2) regular allotments in the budget, and (3) special private, state, or federal grants. It is not always possible to isolate the revenue earmarked especially for evaluating prior learning. Many institutions and programs charge the student an assessment fee which seems to have been arrived at arbitrarily at first and then adjusted as experience was gained. Some institutions and programs charge a flat fee regardless of the number of credits ultimately assigned; others have a fee structure based on the number of credits received or the number of areas of competence to be assessed.

For example, Iona College extracts a blanket administrative fee of $75 specifically for assessing prior learning, regardless of the number of credits given. Edison College, on the other hand, rules that if the evaluation involves more than "one significant body of knowledge and thus more than one examiner," a fee of $75 is charged for each body of knowledge. Since Edison College is an examining institution, it has no faculty of its own and the assessment fee can be tied directly to the number of faculty needed to do the work.

Fordham University uses a scale from a minimum of $50 to a maximum of $200. If a student receives ten credits or less, the charge is $50; eleven to twenty credits, $100; twenty-one to thirty credits, $150; and thirty-one to forty credits, $200. The Fordham system comes as close as any to "charging by the credit." While it is undeniably true that the more credits a student receives, the more it will cost the institution, the "charging by the credit" system should be avoided. Although the process might be academically beyond reproach, the implication of buying credits is unmistakably present.

Although some programs attempt to make adjustments for students who cannot pay the fee, this practice is not common. Administrators report that very few students are unable to pay the assessment fee. This finding is confirmed by students, who state that they do not think the fees charged are exorbitant. Of course, one wonders how many students do not apply because of the cost. Many administrators contend that the student eligible for prior learning assessment is older, employed, fairly well established, and should be able to pay the fees. Perhaps; perhaps not. It is certainly conceivable that the same discriminatory conditions are in effect for the oppressed adult student as for the oppressed younger student. Scholarships should be made available to help students achieve prior learning credits as well as future learning credits. Such action is well in line with the principle of equal access to prior learning credits discussed earlier.

Some state institutions receive an FTE (Full-Time Equivalency) generated budget for the particular special program of which assessing prior learning is a part. Since FTE budgets are normally based on the number of students in a classroom and/ or the student-faculty ratio in a given discipline, they are inappropriate for the individualized assessment of prior learning. Indeed, they are especially inadequate when a total program or institution is devoted to the concept of the learner as central. These outmoded equations are based on normally defined *instructional* time rather than on *learner* time. New formulas need to be devised if nontraditional study is to take its rightful place in the public systems of higher education. These formulas would probably show a slightly higher cost-per-student at the beginning of a program with a steady decrease until the cost stabilized or fell slightly below the "normal" per-student-cost. Such a pattern is typical of most new programs which receive start-up and planning funds. The study currently being conducted by Medsker and his associates (1974) should shed considerable light on the cost of programs and their financial support.

Whatever the funding source, the question of cost must be considered and honestly approached before the process begins. As is true of the other basic decisions discussed in this chapter, the more decision makers—including students—are involved in talking about cost, the more readily acceptable will be the inevitable answer that it *will* cost. Though some programs have begun through grants from private, state, and federal sources, these funds are limited in time and amount. Some of the best programs operating today would not be in existence had it not been for a grant. However, long-range planning, with or without grant funds, demands that a solid financial base be found if the process is to be successful.

Compensation for Faculty

Faculty attitudes toward receiving compensation for crediting prior learning are extremely interesting. It is not surprising that faculty in institutions which treat the assessment of prior learning as an integral part of the program find no rationale for receiving extra compensation for this aspect of their work. Such institutions as Empire State College and Minnesota Metropolitan State College employ faculty as mentors or facilitators, and crediting prior learning is considered merely one aspect of the total job. It *is* surprising to find that almost all faculty members who service special programs feel they should not be compensated for evaluating prior learning. Queens College and Fordham University, for example, have been using regular faculty to assess prior learning for eleven years and four years, respectively. None of the eight professors interviewed at those institutions feels that he or she needs extra compensation for this, either in released time or cash payment. Even in two institutions that do compensate faculty—one in released time and one in cash—some of those faculty did not expect this remuneration. Of the four faculty members interviewed who stated most definitely that they did expect compensation, only one indicated a preference for overload pay; the remaining three preferred released time. When asked whether faculty should be compensated one teacher summed up the feelings of many in his reply: "I do not! I think faculty should be compensated for having a teaching position in the university. I think that a part of their responsibility within their own departmental unit should be to grant life experience credit, to do independent study with students, to teach courses, etc."

Two factors seem to contribute to this faculty attitude.

First of all, for most faculty this is a relatively new and still fresh experience which carries with it the excitement and challenge of working on a one-to-one basis with a new type of student. These feelings are evident in their answers to a question regarding their major satisfaction with the process. As one faculty member puts it, "I'm always intrigued by being able to move out of a traditional realm of learning in providing education. I have seen very gifted people come in and apply for life experience credit. What is heartening to me is that many of these people could be sitting on the other side of the desk. They could be teaching, they could be serving as advisors." Another faculty member states, "I find these students to be atypical of the normal college students. These are people who really want an education, who are willing to listen, to do, to ask questions, and be critical about these. They are willing to analyze things. It's a one-to-one kind of teaching relationship which you really do not find in a large classroom today."

The second factor contributing to the faculty willingness to forego compensation is the number of students each faculty member has to assess in any given semester. Although some professors had assessed a *total* in excess of 150 students, the mean number of students handled per semester was 7.2 with a range of from one to 22. When asked how they would feel if the number of students to assess rose significantly—45 per semester was the hypothetical number used—all stated that then some provision would need to be made for compensation. Almost three-fourths preferred released time to overload cash payment.

It is quite obvious that such a workload would necessitate some reward other than the satisfactions already mentioned. The process is time- and energy-consuming, involving faculty in practices which are new, complex, and without much precedent. The compensation should be consistent with other academic compensation *as should the rewards.* Many faculty mention that while their chairpeople and deans are in favor of the process, assessing prior learning is not properly recognized in considering promotions, salary increases, and tenure, especially in special programs where such crediting is seen as somewhat ancillary. As one faculty member says, "My department chairman thinks it's [assessing prior learning] a great idea and he is all for it so long as it doesn't detract from my regular work."

This attitude toward the many aspects of nontraditional study is all too common among faculty and administrators. Classroom teaching, traditional research, and publications are still the most frequently used criteria in the academic reward system. The respectability of evaluating prior learning will be greater if a maximum number of decision makers are involved from the beginning. The reward depends directly on the respectability *and should also be built in from the beginning.* The nature of the faculty members involved in the process also affects the respectability: full professors as well as instructors from as many academic disciplines as possible should be included.

Chapter III

⨊⨊⨊⨊⨊⨊

Getting Started

Assessing prior learning for academic credit poses unique problems from the very beginning. While most prospective students know that for transfer credit they must submit official transcripts from institutions they have attended, few understand what is needed for the assessment of prior learning. Publicity to prospective students must convey accurately what learning can be credited and what constitutes documentation, and oral information from program staff must also be clear so that misunderstandings are kept to a minimum. This chapter deals with the three initial phases of the process of assessing prior learning: (1) developing necessary forms and records, (2) counseling, and (3) offering prior learning assessment seminars. Not only are these initial phases important because they convey the plan for the total program; they set the tone for the process and for further learning.

Developing Forms and Records

Application Form. The application form and accompanying descriptions of the educational program and the process of assessing prior learning are usually the first written materials received by prospective students. Some institutions prefer to keep these as short as possible, indicating that the student can and will receive more detailed information either upon contacting the institution or once admitted. Others attempt to give the student the entire academic and social rationale of the institution and the program, providing a step-by-step account of how the student will move through the program. There is danger in both extremes. Enough information must be conveyed to inform the prospective student adequately and enough information must be received so that staff can determine whether the program is appropriate for the student and vice versa. When Queens College's Adult Collegiate Education Program (ACE) began in 1963, a thirteen-page application form was devised which asked students everything from where they attended high school to whether or not they held museum subscriptions. The rationale behind this was quite simply that all of this information was necessary to make initial and future decisions with the students. Needless to say, the eagerness to be thorough did more to confuse and alienate prospective students than it did to assist them in planning. The needs of the staff to be secure in this new venture generated much paper and a good deal of unnecessary anxiety for the students. It is gratifying to note that the application for the ACE Program is now down to a manageable four pages. Over the years it was found that some of the information asked for initially was immaterial and some, not essential to the admission process, could be obtained at a later date.

The assessment of prior learning can involve either one or two application forms. If the process is an integral part of the admission procedure, the same form is used usually to admit students to the program and to elicit the initial information necessary for evaluating their previous experiences. If the evaluation is done later, be it a month or a year, separate applications for admission and for assessment are commonly used. In either case, if the program undertakes to credit prior learning, information about the process is sent with the application form, regardless of when the assessment takes place.

It would be impossible to list and/or explain all of the experiences which have the potential for being assessed for credit. It is equally impossible to detail exactly *how* each experience out of which some credit may be garnered will be evaluated. Because the process is highly individualized, the information prepared for dissemination must be specific, yet broad. This requirement is not easily met. Some programs that believe only minimum guidelines are necessary want the process to evolve between students and faculty. Others have a need to be so specific that the prospective student is lost in a sea of jargon, making a decision to enter the program or not almost impossible. The necessity for considering and answering the basic questions I raised earlier becomes quite evident when preparing material to send to prospective students. The clearer the understanding of what is being credited, the more lucid the explanation to prospective students.

The nature of the introductory material sent to students depends, of course, on the nature of the particular institution or program. Below are examples of material from three representative institutions. The first, Iona College, in New Rochelle, New York, represents institutions which have special programs for adults and which feature credit for prior learning as one way to obtain advanced standing (see Exhibit 1). The assessment of prior learning is described in the material entitled "Life Experience Credit." On a special Life Experience form (not included in Exhibit 1) students indicate the courses for which they would like to receive credit. Program officials then reserve the right to delete, or add, after evaluation has taken place. The

EXHIBIT 1

ADMISSIONS APPLICATION FOR DIVISION OF GENERAL STUDIES, IONA COLLEGE (abridged)

(Items 1 through 15—such items as name, address, birthdate, marital status, occupation, high school attendance.)

16. List any NON-COLLEGE CREDIT educational programs, including military programs, in which you have participated, indicating dates.

....

....

EMPLOYMENT-EXPERIENCE

17. Job Title .... Approximate dates of Employment ....

    Employer .... Address ....

....

....

COMMUNITY ACTIVITIES:

18. Describe briefly any community activities in which you have participated or are presently participating, indicating offices held. ....

....

....

SPECIAL INTERESTS:

19. Briefly list special subject-matter interests, avocational, and leisure-time activities. ....

....

....

20. Why are you seeking more education? ....

....

....

Continued on next page

EXHIBIT 1

Continued from previous page

SUPPLEMENTARY FORM FOR ADVANCED STANDING (abridged)

Advanced Standing includes credits towards the degree earned in the following ways:

1. Successful completion of courses taken at another college or postsecondary institute.

2. Work or life experience which can be evaluated for college credit toward the degree.

3. C.L.E.P. Test (College Level Examination Program).

4. C.P.E. (College Proficiency Examinations).

5. U.S.A.F.I. (United States Armed Forces Credit).

Do you plan to take CLEP? .... yes .... no. Expected Date: ....

Do you plan to take CPE? .... yes .... no. Expected Date: ....

Do you plan to take CLEP at Iona? .... yes .... no. Expected Date: ....

Do you plan to take CPE at Iona? .... yes .... no. Expected Date: ....

If you wish to apply for any Advanced Standing credit, please follow these directions:

1. For academic works completed at another college or post-secondary institution, send transcripts to address listed below.

2. Life Experience credit is credit granted upon evaluation of accomplishments and experiences not ordinarily considered part of the traditional academic study. These activities may include professional experiences in business, industry, or the community; organized and supervised volunteer activities; foreign language skills gained through special opportunities or travel; and/or apprenticeship positions. All such experience, however, must relate to your educational goals and will be evaluated in terms of their contribution to learning. For Life Experience Credit, send the following:

   (a) Any literature (brochures, outlines, course descriptions, catalogues, etc.) which describes the activity you have been involved in.

   (b) Write a description of your work and/or volunteer experience. For example: What was your job? Were you a supervisor? Did you have increasing responsibility as time went on? Were you in

Continued on next page

EXHIBIT 1

Continued from previous page

a decision making position? How many people reported to you? Did you help develop or change a program? How many people did you serve? How long were you there? How many hours a week did you work? Did you receive a salary? How did the program or institute change due to your efforts?

(c) Please submit two letters of recommendation for each "Life Experience" activity you wish to have accredited from people who are able to evaluate your contribution.

3. C.L.E.P. Scores.

4. C.P.E. Scores.

5. U.S.A.F.I. Credits.

LIFE EXPERIENCE CREDIT (abridged)

Life Experience Credit is granted upon our evaluation of accomplishments and experiences not ordinarily considered part of the traditional academic study. These activities may include professional experiences in business, industry, or the community; organized and supervised volunteer activities; foreign language skills gained through special opportunities or travel; and/or apprenticeship positions. All such experience, however, should relate to your educational goals.

Remember, you must prove to our satisfaction that you have *learned* from your experiences.

Suggested Procedures for Students Applying for Life Experience Credits.

1. List learning experience which you believe can be translated into academic credit. Among the things you might include are:

a. Self-taught or tutor-taught academic or creative skills such as the mastery of languages, musical instruments, studio arts, writing, etc. How long have you studied? What proof do you have of your mastery, etc.? With whom did you study? What were your tutor's credentials?

b. Organizational experience of either a voluntary or professional nature. What was your job? Were you a supervisor? Did you have increasing responsibility as time went on? Were you in a decision making position? How many people reported to you? Did you help develop or change a program? How many people did you serve? How long were you there? How many hours a week did you work? Did you receive a salary? How did the program or institution change due

Continued on next page

EXHIBIT 1

Continued from previous page

to your efforts? (Proof of leadership ability, initiative, tenacity, sense of purpose, level of responsibility, and scope of work is important here.)

c. In-service or non-credit courses you have taken, for example, courses completed in the armed forces, police or fire department, school systems, voluntary agencies, continuing or adult education programs, courses given to employees of corporations to upgrade skills.

2. Submit all work in *triplicate* to Office of General Studies. (Do not submit originals of items you cannot replace.) We offer you the following help in preparing your portfolios:

a. General Studies conducts at least two Life Experience Seminars each semester for your convenience. At these times you can bring your working papers and rough drafts for discussion.

b. The administrators of General Studies would be available to discuss your life experience petition once it is in progress or outline form.

c. There is a growing library of life experience portfolios available for you to study in the Office of General Studies. These portfolios must be reviewed in the office, however. Please make an appointment to review related portfolios at your convenience.

d. We can give you the names and phone numbers of people who have received Life Experience Credit. You might want to discuss particular problems with them.

---

intention is to allow the student to begin thinking, from the beginning, how experiences might translate into learning and be applied to certain formal courses or other learning events.

The second example, from the University of Wisconsin at Green Bay (UWGB), represents institutions which include the assessment of prior learning as part of the master plan and make the process available to everyone (see Exhibit 2). UWGB

EXHIBIT 2
GUIDELINES, UNIVERSITY OF WISCONSIN AT GREEN BAY

There are 7 steps in the procedure for applying for credit based on experience:

1. Prepare a resume of learning experiences and review it with an academic advisor.

2. Complete the "Credit Based on Experience" form and review it with an academic advisor to identify those experiences which seem most appropriate to present for credit.

3. On a separate sheet, prepare a summary list of the courses and/or programs for which credits are being sought and indicate the total number of credits being sought.

4. Assemble the necessary detailed information and gather the documents which are to be used to verify the experiences identified in Number 2.

5. Review all materials with an academic advisor. If all materials are in excellent form and order and if the student approves, the advisor may send the materials to the appropriate chairperson or faculty member (step 6) and to the University's Evaluation Committee (step 7), eliminating the burden of unnecessarily having to go to additional offices.

6. Consult with an appropriate chairperson or faculty member, if necessary.

7. Present materials and chairperson/faculty recommendations to the University's Evaluation Committee.

Not everything learned in the past will be appropriate for submission and evaluation. For this reason the first two steps in the procedure focus on identifying the learning experiences for which credit is being sought.

Some persons find it difficult to express themselves in writing while others have difficulty with oral communication. That is why the first three steps in the procedure provide an opportunity for both written and oral communication. The process should not be frightening or discouraging for the student but at the same time University personnel should be provided with an additional opportunity to assess communication skills and refer students to the Special Learnings Program Office, if necessary.

Continued on next page

EXHIBIT 2

Continued from previous page

Step number 4 addresses the problem of presenting evidence of learning experiences. Transcripts, displomas, certificates of completion, licenses, examination scores, program descriptions and job descriptions are some of the documents which can be submitted in support of learnings claimed. Some detailed information may need to be gathered or assembled into a format suitable for submission. The basic responsibility for this step rests with the student but academic advisors will help the students who require assistance. (Normally, all materials submitted will be organized in the following way: (1) The "Credit Based on Experience" form, (2) the summary statement, and (3) documentation.)

The review of the materials in step number 5 may point to the need for some performance alternatives such as tests, demonstrations, and portfolios of art work. If they are needed, the academic advisor will assist the students in contacting the persons(s) to whom he/she must be referred.

Step number 6 provides for the direct involvement of chairpersons and faculty members, whose special areas of competence and knowledge are needed in making the evaluation. The responsibility for recommending credit for experience rests with the faculty.

The final step in the procedure is a review of all materials submitted by the student and the recommendations made by the faculty members. The review is conducted by an Evaluation Committee that is appointed by the Dean of the Colleges. Upon completion of the review of the materials and the faculty recommendations, an academic action will be taken and will be signed by the Dean of the Colleges or his designee. The Academic Action Form along with the Credit Based on Experience Form, the summary statement, and the documentation are sent to the Registrar's Office where the action is entered on the student's transcript and the other materials are filed.

---

recognizes the intrinsic value of experiential education and builds both future experiential education events and the possibility of assessment of prior learning into the academic plan of all students. It is one of an extremely small number of institutions that provide evaluation of previous experience for both adult and younger students. Prior learning can be assessed most any time and can include experiential events which occur concurrently with the student's regular program. In this instance, what distinguishes prior learning from regular internships or study abroad programs is that the prior learning events are engaged in without supervision or intervention and, thus, must be assessed *as though* they occurred prior to admission.

The assessment of prior learning at UWGB does not have to be part of the admission process nor does it have to be directly related to future goals. The institution is interested in breadth of academically oriented experience; it recognizes that some people change goals and should not be penalized for doing so. One of the administrators at UWGB gives the example of a man who had quite a bit of advertising business experience and also operated a resort motel. This student's goal now was a degree with emphasis in the literature/language area. The student received some credit for his previous business experience although this was not directly related to his immediate educational goal.

The third set of materials illustrates still another type of institution. Minnesota Metropolitan State College (MMSC) has a totally competence-based curriculum. Both prior and future learning must be related to five areas of competence described in Exhibit 3. There are actually two admission procedures for MMSC. The first admits the student to the college and allows the student to partake in courses and other events. However, this first step does not admit the student to candidacy for the degree. For students to be accepted as degree candidates they must submit an acceptable Draft Degree Pact, which includes both prior learning to be verified and an identification of competences to be gained after admission. Since MMSC is one of the truly "learner as central" programs, it comes closer to incorporating prior and future learning in a total educational program than most others. A careful review of the Draft Degree Pact of "Minerva Metropol," a fictitious person used by MMSC for illustrative purposes for prospective students (see

EXHIBIT 3

FIVE AREAS OF COMPETENCE,
MINNESOTA METROPOLITAN STATE COLLEGE

The five areas of competence which you as a student with the College should address in your draft pact include: basic learning and communications; personal growth and social awareness; civic; recreational; and vocational.

Communications and Basic Learning Competence

For all educated individuals it is necessary to be both an effective receiver and skillful sender of information. It is the hope of this institution that as a student you share our wish to see yourself acting as a fully functioning self-directed learner. There are a number of areas where you can set goals which will assist you in achieving competence as a communicator. Messages may be written, oral, pictorial, or nonverbal, and you may need to demonstrate competence in more than one or in all of these modes. There are also symbol systems or languages which you can learn—standard English, colloquial English, technical English, musical notation, color and forms, textured materials, body language and movement, mathematics, statistics, accounting, computer languages such as fortran and cobol, and foreign languages such as Spanish, Japanese, and Russian. The specific symbol systems which you must master will be determined by your personal, vocational, and other goals. In short, learning to communicate effectively will be a part of almost everything else you do. Every learning activity you engage in will require you to be either an effective creator or an effective interpreter of communications.

Personal Development and Social Awareness

This is a most important skill for a self-directed learner. It is the ability to look at oneself, to identify one's strengths and limitations, to be able purposefully to set goals as a result of taking inventory, and to plan and carry out strategies which make possible the realization of those goals. Knowledge of social patterns, mores, and customs of one's own background and the backgrounds of others can be an integral part of the social awareness component of this competence. The knowledge you possess of groups and individuals and how they function will help you to clarify your own values. In a similar way clarification of your own values will help you to

Continued on next page

EXHIBIT 3

Continued from previous page

understand and evaluate others. There are numerous strategies which you can employ to understand yourself and others.

Civic Competence

This is an ability to be consciously conceptual and an active participant in community affairs. The decisions made by communities are neither entirely "political" nor related solely to government. There is a wide array of activities of secular and nonsecular voluntary groups which enables the student as citizen to contribute to the civic process. Knowledge and analysis of economic, cultural, religious, and social decisions make possible informed participation in the civic process. Understanding can be gained either while participating or as preparation for involvement in civic activities. We believe that MMSC should assist its students to become self-governing members of their communities: to become citizens in the classic sense of the term.

Recreational Competence

The ability to explore new interests and activities and enlarge on old ones so that one constantly can draw on these resources for continued growth and enrichment of one's quality of life. This competence is particularly important as vocational and family roles diminish in each individual's life. For most of us, intermingled with our vocational obligations is our additional need for recreation and renewal. As our society moves toward the 35-hour or four-day work week and is forced to reexamine the role and meaning of work, it behooves you to prepare for the changes in life-style such developments imply.

Vocational Competence

Although MMSC is an undergraduate liberal arts college, we believe that no one should be granted a bachelor's degree who does not have competence in some vocation—a profession, trade, or occupation. It is essential that you have the knowledge and skills necessary to be a useful and productive person, not only for economic independence but also for reasons of self-esteem and satisfaction. You should be able to move occupationally within an increasingly unstable job market. The choice of which vocation you pursue is entirely your own as is the responsibility for securing a particular position. Even if you enter the college already qualified in a particular vocation you may desire a secondary vocational competence. If your vocational competences are too specialized, you may need to broaden your understanding of your vocation and its relation to contemporary society.

Exhibit 4), reveals that Part I contains the competences to be verified prior to admission to degree candidacy and describes the prior learning to be assessed and credited. Part II illustrates the competences to be gained after admission to degree candidacy. Both parts detail the strategies to be used to verify prior and future learning as well as naming the competences. The

---

EXHIBIT 4

GUIDELINES FOR PREPARING DRAFT DEGREE PACT, MINNESOTA METROPOLITAN STATE COLLEGE

The attached draft degree pact has been formulated to give the students in the course in Individualized Educational Planning an idea of what a degree pact might look like. The educational plan implied by this pact is probably over-ambitious, perhaps even unrealistic. The value of this hypothetical pact lies mainly in being a presentation of specific competences related to one person's life goals and the presentation of specific competence statements. The reader should note that some competence statements are very specific, while others are rather general in terms of what the student intends to do. Hopefully, these samples will convey to the reader the idea that the total degree pact should relate to his overall life plan and that the student may be able to write some competence goals in very specific terms while others will appear only in skeleton form (hopefully to be "fleshed out" at a later date).

The story of Minerva Metropol is that she received an A.A. Degree from Metropolitan Community College in June 1954 at the age of 20. She married soon after that and began to raise a family. For a number of years she worked part-time in the Girl Scout organization and served as a volunteer in a number of civic organizations. She also acquired a number of secretarial skills during this time and in February 1971, at the age of 37, she entered Minnesota Metropolitan State College with two life goals in mind: (1) to prepare for work as a caseworker in women's correctional institutions; (2) improve her general capability in expressing herself.

Continued on next page

EXHIBIT 4

Continued from previous page

CRITERIA FOR REVIEW OF DRAFT DEGREE PACT OF
APPLICANTS FOR CANDIDACY

To be admitted to candidacy, the individual must prepare a draft
of a Degree Pact consisting of the following elements:

A statement of the eighteen specific competences which will fulfill
the student's education goals and would be listed on the student's Official
Transcript. The competences must conform to the technical definition of
competence. At least one competence must be included in each of the competence areas referred to in Tenet IV. The number of competences listed
may be reduced at the rate of one competence per five quarter hours above
the 90 accepted for admission purposes, except that the draft Degree Pact
must list a minimum of nine competences.

A statement of the learning strategies the student would undertake
to achieve any of the competences not already possessed.

A statement of the types of evidence the student would offer (including tests and other measuring techniques to be employed), to prove,
demonstrate, or verify that the student possesses the claimed competence.
Such evidence *must conform to standards for adequate evidence.*

A brief statement by the student indicating the relationship of the
eighteen specific competences to one or more life goals, which life goal or
goals shall also be set forth in writing and attached to the Draft Degree
Pact.

DRAFT DEGREE PACT OF MINERVA METROPOL (abridged)*

PART I.   Competences to be Verified Prior to Admission to Degree
Candidacy

   A.   COMMUNICATION AND BASIC LEARNING
        COMPETENCES

        1. *Title of competence:*
           Knows and can apply basic principles of conducting an in-
           dividual interview.

           Process by which competence was gained
           Read three books on theory and methodology of conducting
           an individual interview and the related processes of managing

---

* The documents pertaining to Minerva Metropol were developed by the
staff of the college and are the property of MMSC. The content of the material
is currently being revised, and should be viewed primarily in terms of its form.

Continued on next page

EXHIBIT 4

Continued from previous page

a volunteer organization, personnel selection and supervision, and program development. Served as a part-time Assistant to the Council Administrator (name) of the Girl Scouts, interviewing prospective volunteer workers.

Description of evidence to be used to assess competence

Was observed by three office supervisors in the process of interviewing. A standard rating form will be completed and a judgment made by three examiners. Expect to verify the following:

a. I can easily establish rapport with various types of people.

b. I am able to elicit all required information.

c. I can probe without creating resistance on part of subject.

d. I communicate clearly the responsibilities of volunteer position and Girl Scout policies and procedures.

B. CIVIC COMPETENCES

1. *Title of competence*

Knows the role and function of Girl Scout, Camp Fire, and 4-H programs and their effects on girls in preparing them for citizenship roles.

Process by which competence was gained

Read literature, including histories and research reports, relative to the effectiveness of the Girl Scout, Camp Fire, and 4-H programs in preparing participants for citizenship roles. Has interviewed fifty former members of the Girl Scout program who are now adults and live in the Twin Cities.

Description of evidence to be used to assess competence

Prepare a fifty-page paper on the effects of the Girl Scout, Camp Fire, and 4-H programs in preparing participants for citizenship roles. Submit paper to three expert evaluators who read paper and conduct an oral examination. Evaluation statement should indicate knowledge level equivalent to a chapter leader of these groups.

2. *Title of competence*

Knows and can apply the basic techniques of fund raising for a civic organization.

Continued on next page

EXHIBIT 4

Continued from previous page

Process by which competence was gained

Over a period of ten years, served as a volunteer in the annual United Fund drive. Progressed from the level of worker to team captain to central office staff. In the central office, supervised organizing of volunteers, wrote press releases, conducted volunteer training sessions, and served on the citizens council when she participated in the decision making process relative to organizing and supervising campaigns.

Description of evidence to be used to assess competence

In a fifteen-page paper, articulate the basic theory and methodology of the United Fund approach to fund raising. The director of the central office and the chairman of the citizens council will verify that I know the literature and history of the organization and its role in the community. Their report on my efficiency at the various levels of the organization should indicate a performance level rating me in the top 20% of volunteer personnel attached to the United Fund.

C. VOCATIONAL COMPETENCES

1. *Title of competence*

Knows and can apply concepts and skills related to production typewriting, reproduction processes, and office supervision.

Process by which competence was gained

Successfully completed three related courses requiring thirty contact hours each in production typewriting, reproduction, and office supervision at the Twin Cities Business College.

Description of evidence to be used to assess competence

Observed by three office supervisors in the process of typing, reproduction of materials, and supervision of office personnel. A standard rating form will be completed and a judgment made by the three examiners. Summary of the rating form should indicate the following:

a. Normal typing speed is 80 w.p.m.

b. Can efficiently use reproduction machines and make appropriate selection of reproduction process relative to assigned tasks.

Continued on next page

EXHIBIT 4

Continued from previous page

   c. Effectively organizes tasks, communicates expectations to subordinates, and objectively evaluates work of subordinates.

2. *Title of competence*
   Knows the basic concepts and fundamental information relative to deviant human behavior.

   Process by which competence was gained
   Read three standard textbooks and six related books in the general subject area of deviant human behavior including: Abnormal Psychology and Modern Life (Coleman), Abnormal Psychology, Changing Conceptions (Zax, Melvin and Cower), The Abnormal Personality (White), Outline of Psychoanalysis (Freud). Books were recommended by psychologist-friend (name) and informal conversations were conducted between student and psychologist-friend on content of books.

   Description of evidence to be used to assess competence
   Will be given a standard final examination used for level course in abnormal psychology.

PART II.   Competences Gained After Admission to Degree Candidacy

A. COMMUNICATION AND
   BASIC LEARNING COMPETENCES

1. *Title of competence*
   Knows and can apply the basic principles of reducing information written in technical language to language that will make the information usable by lay volunteer workers in a human services area.

   Process by which competence is to be gained
   Serve a two-month internship at a human services agency, read basic text on simplified writing and translate basic texts as well as a basic procedural manual for professionals into an inservice training manual to be used in upgrading the skills of the volunteer workers associated with the Agency.

   Description of evidence to be used to assess competence
   Final draft of the manual to be evaluated by a panel of 3

Continued on next page

EXHIBIT 4

Continued from previous page

persons. Expect to produce a valuable and understandable inservice training manual.

B. CIVIC COMPETENCES

1. *Title of competence*

Knows and can apply the basic standards of pollution control.

Process by which competence is to be gained

Through independent study project, read basic federal and state guideline documents, study research reports on an area of Minneapolis, make observations and elementary measurements of the area, and write a report which applies standards to the area of analyzing current circumstances and making recommendations.

Description of evidence to be used to assess competence

Report to be read and evaluated by the project supervisor. His review should indicate that I know the basic standards of pollution control and can appropriately apply those standards in an evaluation of the environmental quality of an area.

C. VOCATIONAL COMPETENCES

1. *Title of competence*

Knows and can apply various approaches to sensitivity training.

Process by which competence is to be gained

Through active participation in simulation games and resulting discussions, will acquire knowledge and learn to apply competitive, noninteractive, encounter, and cooperative approaches to sensitivity training.

Description of evidence to be used to assess competence

On the basis of quantitative outcomes of participation in the simulation games, evaluation by the other participants and observations made by two psychologists, I expect to be able to:

a. accurately predict how others will evaluate me on a number of personality traits.

Continued on next page

EXHIBIT 4

Continued from previous page

b. accurately evaluate the personality traits of other people.
c. recognize social actions and their consequences.
d. recognize the need for a qualified trainer for sensitivity training groups.

2. *Title of competence*
Knows and can apply basic procedures as a counselor of individuals.

Process by which competence is to be gained
Enroll in a group learning opportunity in fundamentals of counseling, or use supervised independent study.

Description of evidence to be used to assess competence
Will be observed by a panel of three experienced counselors, selected by an instructor, conducting a counseling session. A rating form will be used by the three judges to assess my counseling competence. I expect to be able to:
a. show genuine empathy in responses to client behavior.
b. help client to rationally analyze problems.
c. help client to formulate possible solutions to problems and help client to evaluate these options.
d. elicit client satisfaction.

3. *Title of competence*
Knows the basic differences in sexual behavioral responses between human males and females.

Process by which competence is to be gained
Enroll in and successfully complete a group learning opportunity in human sexual behavior or evolve and complete a reading list.

Description of evidence to be used to assess competence
Obtain a satisfactory score on an essay test constructed and scored by an instructor.

4. *Title of competence*
Knows the structure and function of the various types of correctional institutions in the U.S.A.

Process by which competence is to be gained
Enroll in and successfully complete the group learning op-

Continued on next page

EXHIBIT 4

Continued from previous page

portunity in penal systems or evolve and complete a reading list.

Description of evidence to be used to assess competence
Obtain a satisfactory score on an objective test constructed by an instructor.

5. *Title of competence*
Knows basic procedures used in correctional institutions.

Process by which competence is to be gained
Complete readings drawn from a list jointly compiled with an expert. I will conduct interviews of staff personnel, guards and inmates at a prison. Once a week, I will meet with expert to discuss readings and content of interviews.

Description of evidence to be used to assess competence
According to a general outline not given to me in advance, a panel of 2 will ask questions. I expect the two evaluators will judge that I have a thorough knowledge of all the basic correctional procedures.

6. *Title of competence*
Knows and can apply knowledge of the operation of a half-way house for women ex-offenders.

Process by which competence is to be gained
Work as a volunteer staff member at a half-way house for a three month period. Be responsible for helping women adjust to release from corrections institution via group counseling sessions, job placement and referral to appropriate community agencies. Work alongside regular staff.

Description of evidence to be used to assess competence
Be observed by staff members in referral work.
Be able to:

a. adjust quickly to working as member of house team and demonstrate ability to work with women at the house.

b. demonstrate understanding of the referral process and those agencies appropriate to house functions, i.e. County Welfare, food stamps, vocational training, job placement, etc.

c. understand the procedures of the house and its role as a half-way house for women parolees and as a diversionary service for women in trouble.

Continued on next page

EXHIBIT 4

Continued from previous page

7. *Title of competence*

Knows and can apply knowledge of the role and function of a caseworker within a women's reformatory.

Process by which competence is to be gained

Serve as an intern at a women's reformatory for a three month period. Read various state policy and procedure manuals from Department of Corrections. Serve two months as a casework aide working with a full-time caseworker.

Description of evidence to be used to assess competence

Be observed by the Supervisor of Casework and one of the caseworkers in the performance of various functions:

a. relating with staff in staff meetings and demonstrating knowledge of various roles caseworker plays—coach, parent, authority figure, etc.

b. demonstrating basic understanding of various functions performed by caseworker in institutional setting of Department of Corrections including education and rehabilitation.

c. establishing rapport with women inmates of lower socioeconomic status than my own.

d. demonstrating basic awareness of policies and procedures of the reformatory and its relationship to the department of correction.

Draft Degree Pact becomes the application for admission to candidacy for the degree. Thus, it can be seen readily that the assessment of prior learning is an integral part of the admission process, as well as a central element in the total educational plan. Once the student is admitted to candidacy, the Degree Pact can be altered by mutual consent of faculty and student.

58   Awarding College Credit for Non-College Learning

As portions of the Pact are completed they are entered on the transcript with the date evaluation was completed and the date the information was entered on the transcript.

Internal Records. Internal records are those evidences of achievement which an institution keeps to record a student's progress through an educational program. Transcripts are those recorded achievements which an institution shares with the larger community. Both present unique challenges when a program embarks on the assessment of prior learning. Internal records pose their own special problems. They must be complete enough to justify that which is posted on the transcript and yet must also be manageable. In the example of the two suitcases full of documentation cited earlier, what should be kept? No institution has the storage space to amass the voluminous documentation presented by many students. Part of the problem lies in inadequate counseling of students and faculty as to what is relevant and what is embellishment. Another source of difficulty is the insecurity of administrators who must save *everything* in case the accreditation team asks for it. Even after solving these problems, however, assessing prior learning still generates more "data per credit" than does transfer credit or credit by standardized examinations. It would help to have the faculty and recordkeeping staff discuss this issue before the process begins. Statutes of limitations in most institutions detail how long all conceivable kinds of records need be kept. Internal records relating to the evaluation of prior learning are those "proofs" or documents which certify what appears on the transcript. These need not be kept any longer than faculty normally would keep final examination papers. Furthermore, it is often possible to keep the internal records down to a manageable size if only one document per learning event is kept. Many learning events are verified by three or four items, a number which seems unnecessary. Finally, many of the internal records can and should be on microfilm.

Transcripts. Whenever the word *transcript* is used in connection with assessing prior learning, the inevitable question is raised, "But what will the graduate schools do with this? How will they interpret 'Life Experience—10 credits'?" There are a number of issues in this question which must be considered separately. Future-oriented experiential education, such as a directed internship, poses problems in certain disciplines but not in others. For example, a transcript forwarded to a graduate school of social work from an accredited undergraduate social work program which has the following entry will not be questioned: "Field Work I—10 credits." The graduate school understands the accrediting standards of the Council on Social Work Education for undergraduate programs as these standards relate to field work. The graduate school understands that the student has had at least the minimum number of clock hours of properly supervised field instruction. Furthermore, the graduate school also knows that the student's undergraduate folder (not submitted to the graduate school) has a supervisor's evaluation of that student's field work performance. The graduate school also knows that it can request a copy of that evaluation. The same could be said of an entry which read, "Practice Teaching—10 credits."

As a matter of fact, most professional graduate schools have dealt with experiential education for so long that the *quality* of directed internships at the undergraduate level is rarely questioned. As long as the "clock-hour" requirement has been met, they usually assume that the quality was acceptable if the student received a passing grade. The assumption is that the undergraduate educator is operating with the same set of standards as the graduate educator. However, graduate programs in the liberal arts are more reluctant to accept certain experiential education events because internships, field work, and direct practice are newcomers. Other aspects of experiential education, such as independent study, directed readings, or study-abroad programs, are more accepted because they look more like traditional education and they have been around longer.

Prior learning credits, regardless of discipline, pose problems because they are new, are not yet in mass use, and are not standardized or sanctioned by the professional or educational accrediting associations. Therefore, many programs attempt to disguise prior learning credits or convert them directly to course credits for use on the transcript. These devices, admittedly, are easier for everyone, including the student, to deal with but ultimately will cause harm because they continue to silently admit that the process is shady. The student's transcript should be an accurate account of what the student has accomplished, not what one college thinks another would like to know. Nontraditional study often becomes very traditional when confronted with the transcript. Experimental designs are forced into traditional frames, pressure which makes each lose its identity and often confuses the issue even further. Unless prior learning is handled honestly in the transcript, it will remain suspect in the eyes of those for whom the transcript is intended, be that a graduate school or employer.

Almost all programs report that their eligible students were accepted into graduate school. Some had problems because of the uniqueness of the program. However, these difficulties were solved by correspondence or telephone calls. *In no instance could an administrator honestly say that students were denied admission to a graduate school because they received credit for prior learning.* It almost seems as though the graduate school, like the accrediting association, is used as an excuse for not granting credit for prior learning.

Following are transcripts from two institutions, Florida International University External Degree Program and Minnesota Metropolitan State College.

The Florida International University (FIU) External Degree transcript (Exhibit 5) identifies life/work experience by short descriptions of each experience with inclusive dates. In this case five separate experiences are given a grand total of 30 credits. The number of credits awarded to each experience is not specified. The FIU External Degree Program transcript is a condensation of the Educational Contract signed by the student and his advisor at the beginning of the student's course of study. At FIU crediting prior learning is part of the admission process.

Exhibit 6 is the transcript of "Minerva Metropol," whose Degree Pact was discussed earlier in this chapter. As can be seen by comparing the Pact and the transcript, the transcript verifies what Minerva had set out for herself in the Degree Pact. The MMSC transcript is a good example of a "narrative transcript."

EXHIBIT 5
STUDENT TRANSCRIPT,
FLORIDA INTERNATIONAL UNIVERSITY

Department Number	ID	Course Title	Type	Grade	Credit Earned Quarter Hours
		Advanced Standing:			
		Miami-Dade Community College,			
		Miami, Fl., 1969–1971			94.5
		Associate of Arts			
		degree granted 12–18–71			
		TOTAL			94.5
		Life/Work Experience:			
		Controller, Southern Tackle			
		Company, Miami, Fl., 1972–Present			
		Controller/Accountant, Realty			
		Management Co., Miami, Fl. 1971–72			
		Public Accountant, Self Employed,			
		Miami, Fl., 1965–Present			
		Accountant, Puerto Rico			
		Pharmaceuticals, Inc., Puerto Rico;			
		Virgin Islands, 1962–1965			
		United States Air Force, 1962			
		TOTAL			30.0
		Independent Study:			
Eco. 460		Undergraduate Tutorial	CR		5.0
Eco. 560		Advanced Individual Study	CR		5.5
		TOTAL			10.5
		Formal Coursework:			
His. 420		Jewish Strategy for Survival		B	5.0
Eco. 528		Labor Economics		NC	.0
Mas. 321		Math for Management, Social			
		Sciences I		C	5.0
Eco. 307		Theory of Price		C	5.0
His. 518		Economic Forces in History		B	5.0
Eco. 308		Aggregate Economic Theory		C	5.0
His. 306		Topics in European History		A	5.0
Eco. 312		Development of Economic Thought		C	5.0
His. 460		Labor History		C	5.0
Eco. 321		Regional Economics		C	5.0
		TOTAL			45.0
		Summary:			
		Advanced Standing			94.5
		Life/Work Experience			30.0
		Independent Study			10.5
		Formal Coursework			45.0
		TOTAL			180.0
		B.A. in Economics Degree			
		Granted 12–15–73			

EXHIBIT 6

OFFICIAL TRANSCRIPT OF MINERVA METROPOL,
MINNESOTA METROPOLITAN STATE COLLEGE (abridged)

EXPLANATION

The MMCS student is charged with the responsibility of designing his or her own educational program based on the demonstration of competence(s). The Official Transcript is written by the student under the supervision of the Office of Learning Development. This record indicates: (I) credits transferred from postsecondary institutions; (II) licenses and certificates gained prior to admission to MMSC; (III) formal courses and formal learning activities in which student participated after admission to degree candidacy; (IV) competences gained prior to admission to degree candidacy; and (V) competences gained after admission to degree candidacy.

Students are admitted to degree candidacy after: (1) possessing an Associate Degree, *or* completing the equivalent of 90 quarter or 60 semester hours of post-secondary work, *or* demonstrating a level of competence equivalent to two years of college gained through self-education, on-the-job training, work experience, etc.; and (2) giving adequate evidence of knowing, being able to apply, and being able to evaluate the educational concepts and procedures of MMSC, including the formulation of a Degree Pact (Educational Plan).

As used in the technical sense, the term "competence" means *the ability to exhibit the level of performance that is requisite to the successful attainment of a particular goal.* A student proves, demonstrates, or verifies that he/she has this ability by referring to an assessment of his/her behavior (including that which is written or said). The behavior is *not* the competence but should be an *indication,* to qualified observers, that the specific competence exists and that in an educated judgment it would exist over time. Three levels of competence may be identified, and these are in order of complexity:

26.31 Knowing. To know means to have learned and retained, and to be able to recall, the theory and methodology; or the history and literature; the applicability; and the context of a discipline in relation to a particular competence.

26.32 Applying. To apply means to be able and willing to *use* the theory and methodology; or the history and literature; and context of a

Continued on next page

EXHIBIT 6

Continued from previous page

discipline in new situations as well as routine ones and to be able and willing to analyze relationships, including similarities and differences, in relation to a particular competence.

26.33. Evaluating. To evaluate means to be able to judge the value of a particular competence, that is, the value of the theory and methodology; or the history and literature; the applicability; and the context of a discipline in relation to a goal or stated criteria. This evaluation process implies an informed judgment; one that is grounded in the knowing and applying levels of performance, with the additional ability to support that judgment by rational argument and the discriminating use of evidence.

For a student to have a particular competence listed on his/her Official Transcript, the student must offer adequate evidence to prove, demonstrate, or verify that he/she, at the minimum, possesses a particular competence at the level of *knowing*. When adequate evidence is offered, the college will record that a student possesses competence at the level of applying or evaluating.

Within this transcript competence statements are distributed among five competence areas: (1) communication and basic learning, (2) responsibilities of a self-governing member of a self-governing community, (3) vocation, (4) recreation, (5) personal development and social awareness.

I. CREDITS TRANSFERRED FROM POSTSECONDARY INSTITUTIONS, PRIOR TO ADMISSION TO DEGREE CANDIDACY

Institution	Dates Attended	Credit Transferred
Metropolitan Community College	9/52–6/54	90 quarter hrs. A.A. degree

II. LICENSES AND CERTIFICATES GAINED PRIOR TO ADMISSION TO DEGREE CANDIDACY

Title	Date Awarded
*Production Typist	8/8/59
*Information Reproduction Processor	9/2/59
*Office Supervisor	12/15/59
*Twin Cities Business College	

III. FORMAL COURSES AND FORMAL LEARNING ACTIVITIES IN WHICH STUDENT PARTICIPATED AFTER ADMISSION TO DEGREE CANDIDACY

A. 1. *Title:* Individualized Educational Planning.

Continued on next page

EXHIBIT 6

Continued from previous page

2. *Description:* Basic concepts and procedures of MMSC: competence-based, community-based, student-designed education.
3. *Learning Strategy:* Lectures, group discussions, drafting of a degree pact.
4. *Sponsoring Institution:* MMSC
5. *Dates of Participation:* 3/1/71–4/14/71
6. *Name of Instructors:*

B. 1. *Title:* Fundamentals of Counseling.
2. *Description:* Survey of basic theories and procedures in counseling individuals.
3. *Learning Strategy:* Readings, class discussion, and co-counseling with experienced counselors.
4. *Sponsoring Institution:* MMSC
5. *Dates of Participation:* 6/2/71–7/28/71.
6. *Name of Instructor:*

C. 1. *Title:* Human Sexual Response.
2. *Description:* A study of sexual behavior of human males and females.
3. *Learning Strategy:* Readings, class discussion and a research paper.
4. *Sponsoring Institution:* MMSC
5. *Dates of Participation:* 9/4/71–10/30/71.
6. *Name of Instructor:*

D. 1. *Title:* Penal Systems
2. *Description:* The structure and function of the various types of correctional institutions in the U.S.A.
3. *Learning Strategy:* Readings, class discussions, field trips and a research paper.
4. *Sponsoring Institution:* MMSC
5. *Dates of Participation:* 11/1/71–12/22/71.
6. *Name of Instructor:*

E. 1. *Title:* Correctional Procedures
2. *Description:* Basic procedures used in correctional institutions for women.
3. *Learning Strategy:* Readings, tutorials, interviews.
4. *Sponsoring Institution:* MMSC
5. *Dates of Participation:* 1/15/72–3/29/72.
6. *Name of Tutor:*

Continued on next page

EXHIBIT 6

Continued from previous page

F. 1. *Title:* Advanced Metal Sculpture.
2. *Description:* Modeling, carving and casting individually.
3. *Learning Strategy:* Student works in studio under guidance of instructor—6 hours per week.
4. *Sponsoring Institution:* MMSC
5. *Dates of Participation:* 4/2/72–5/28/72.
6. *Name of Instructor:*
G. 1. *Title:* Pollution Control
2. *Description:* Independent study project with special reference to Minnehaha Parkway area of Minneapolis.
3. *Learning Strategy:* Readings and observations.
4. *Sponsoring Institution:* MMSC
5. *Dates of Participation:* 5/2/72–6/5/72.
6. *Name of Tutor:*
H. 1. *Title:* Divorce Education
2. *Description:* Two-month internship at Twin Cities Divorce Education Center developing an in-service training manual.
3. *Learning Strategy:* Internship and readings.
4. *Sponsoring Institution:* MMSC
5. *Dates of Participation:* 8/1/72–9/30/72.
6. *Name of Supervisor:*
I. 1. *Title:* Casework in an Institutional Setting.
2. *Description:* Internship as aide to caseworker in Shakopee Women's Reformatory.
3. *Learning Strategy:* Internship.
4. *Sponsoring Institution:* MMSC
5. *Dates of Participation:* 1/3/73–3/26/73.
6. *Name of Supervisor:*

IV. COMPETENCES GAINED PRIOR TO ADMISSION TO DEGREE CANDIDACY
A. COMMUNICATION AND BASIC LEARNING COMPETENCES

1. *Title of competence:*
Knows and can apply basic principles of conducting an individual interview.
Process by which competence was gained
Read three books on theory and methodology of conducting an individual interview and the related processes of managing a volunteer organization, personnel selection and super-

Continued on next page

EXHIBIT 6

Continued from previous page

vision, and program development. Served as a part-time Assistant to the Council Administrator (name) of the Girl Scouts, interviewing prospective volunteer workers.

Description of evidence of competence

Was observed by three office supervisors (names) in the process of interviewing. A standard rating form was completed and a judgment made by the three examiners (names). A summary of the rating form indicates the following:

a. student easily establishes rapport with various types of people.

b. student is able to elicit all required information.

c. student can probe without creating resistance on part of subject.

d. student communicates clearly the responsibilities of volunteer position and Girl Scout policies and procedures.

Evaluation completed 4/15/71 and recorded on the transcript 4/21/71.

B. CIVIC COMPETENCES

1. *Title of competence*

Knows the role and function of Girl Scout, Camp Fire, and 4-H programs and their effects on girls in preparing them for citizenship roles.

Process by which competence was gained

Read literature, including histories and research reports, relative to the effectiveness of the Girl Scout, Camp Fire, and 4-H programs in preparing participants for citizenship roles. Has interviewed 50 former members of the Girl Scout program who are now adults and live in the Twin Cities.

Description of evidence of competence

Prepared a 50-page paper on the effects of the Girl Scout, Camp Fire and 4-H programs in preparing participants for citizenship roles. Submitted paper to 3 expert evaluators (names and titles) who read paper and conducted an oral examination. Selected evaluation statements follow:

"Minerva demonstrated a knowledge of the organizations studied equivalent to that possessed by the typical dis-

Continued on next page

EXHIBIT 6

Continued from previous page

trict supervisor of the Girl Scout program."—Georgia Smith, Council Administrator, Twin Cities Council, Girl Scouts.

"She knows as much about the role and function of 4-H citizenship programs as most of our chapter leaders."— Tom Jones, Leader, White Bear 4-H Club.

"We have circulated the report compiled by Mrs. Metropol to all our district supervisors. There is much of interest to us in these findings."—Jane Doe, Ass't National Director, Camp Fire Girls of America."

Evaluation completed 4/15/71 and recorded on the transcript 4/21/71.

2. *Title of competence*

Knows and can apply the basic techniques of fund raising for a civic organization.

Process by which competence was gained

Over a period of ten years, served as a volunteer in the annual United Fund drive. Progressed from the level of worker to team captain to central office staff. In the central office, supervised organizing of volunteers, wrote press releases, conducted volunteer training sessions, and served on the citizens council when she participated in the decision making process relative to organizing and supervising campaigns.

Description of evidence of competence

Was able, in a fifteen-page paper, to articulate the basic theory and methodology of the United Fund approach to fund raising. The director of the central office (name) and the chairman of the citizens council (name) have verified that she knows the literature and history of the organization and its role in the community. Their reports on her efficiency at the various levels of the organization indicate a performance level rating her in the top 20 percent of volunteer personnel attached to the United Fund.

Evaluation completed 4/15/71 and recorded on the transcript 4/21/71.

C. VOCATIONAL COMPETENCES

1. *Title of competence*

Knows and can apply concepts and skills related to produc-

Continued on next page

EXHIBIT 6

Continued from previous page

tion typewriting, reproduction processes, and office supervision.

Process by which competence was gained
Successfully completed three related courses requiring 30 contact hours each in production typewriting, reproduction and office supervision at the Twin Cities Business College.

Description of evidence of competence
Observed by three office supervisors (names) in the process of typing, reproduction of materials and supervision of office personnel. A standard rating form was completed and a judgment made by the three examiners. Summary of the rating form indicates the following:
a. Normal typing speed is 80 w.p.m.
b. Can efficiently use reproduction machines and make appropriate selection of reproduction process relative to assigned tasks.
c. Effectively organizes tasks, communicates expectations to subordinates, and objectively evaluates work of subordinates.
Evaluation completed 4/15/71 and recorded on the transcript 4/21/71.

2. *Title of competence*
Knows the basic concepts and fundamental information relative to deviant human behavior.

Process by which competence was gained
Read three standard textbooks and six related books in the general subject area of deviant human behavior including: Abnormal Psychology and Modern Life (Coleman), Abnormal Psychology, Changing Conceptions (Zax, Melvin and Cower), The Abnormal Personality (White), Outline of Psychoanalysis (Freud). Books were recommended by psychologist-friend (name) and informal conversations were conducted between student and psychologist-friend on content of books.

Description of evidence of competence
Requested and was given a standard final examination used for the upper-level course in abnormal psychology at Hamline University. Instructor (name) of the course reported that

Continued on next page

EXHIBIT 6

Continued from previous page

student received a score on the examination equivalent to that normally obtained by students receiving a "C" or "B" in the course.
Evaluation completed 4/15/71 and recorded on the transcript 4/21/71.

V. COMPETENCES GAINED AFTER ADMISSION TO DEGREE CANDIDACY

A. COMMUNICATION AND BASIC LEARNING COMPETENCES

1. *Title of competence*
Knows and can apply the basic principles of reducing information written in technical language to language that will make the information usable by lay volunteer workers in a human services area.

Process by which competence was gained
While serving a two-month internship at the Twin Cities Divorce Education Center, read basic text on simplified writing and was assigned the task of translating basic texts on divorce education as well as a basic procedural manual for professionals into an inservice training manual to be used in upgrading the skills of the voluntary workers associating with the Center. Was supervised by the Director of the Center (name).

Description of evidence of competence
Final draft of the manual was evaluated by the Director of the Center, one volunteer worker, and an MMSC teacher of writing (names). Their summary evaluation was that "the product was and is a very valuable and understandable inservice training manual."
Evaluation completed 9/30/72 and recorded on the transcript 10/3/72.

B. CIVIC COMPETENCES

1. *Title of competence*
Knows and can apply the basic standards of pollution control.

Process by which competence was gained
Through independent study project supervised by Minnesota State Environmental Control Ass't Dir. (name), read basic

Continued on next page

EXHIBIT 6

Continued from previous page

federal and state guideline documents, studied research reports on the Minnehaha Parkway area of Minneapolis, made observations and elementary measurements of the area, and wrote a report for the MSEC, which applied standards to the area by analyzing current circumstances and making recommendations.

Description of evidence of competence
Report was read and evaluated by the project supervisor (name) and in his review said: "She does know the basic standards of pollution control and did appropriately apply those standards in an evaluation of the environmental quality of the Minnehaha Parkway area."
Evaluation completed 6/3/72 and recorded on the transcript 6/9/72.

C. VOCATIONAL COMPETENCES

1. *Title of competence*
   Knows and can apply various approaches to sensitivity training.

   Process by which competence was gained
   Through active participation with five other students in five simulation games (Interaction, Insight, Personalysis, The Games People Play and Process) and resulting discussions, acquired knowledge and learned to apply competitive, noninteractive, encounter, and cooperative approaches to sensitivity training.

   Description of evidence of competence
   On the basis of quantitative outcomes of participation in the simulation games, evaluation by the other five students, and observations made by two psychologists (names), was judged competent to:
   a. accurately predict how others will evaluate her on a number of personality traits.
   b. accurately evaluate the personality traits of other people.
   c. recognize social actions and their consequences.
   d. recognize the need for a qualified trainer for sensitivity training groups.
   Evaluation completed 5/30/71 and recorded on the transcript 6/2/71.

Continued on next page

EXHIBIT 6

Continued from previous page

2. *Title of competence*

Knows and can apply basic procedures as a counseler of individuals.

Process by which competence was gained

Enrolled in and successfully completed the group learning opportunity in Fundamentals of Counseling, taught by .... Readings and class participation were required, as well as co-counseling with experienced workers.

Description of evidence of competence

In a room that provides a one-way window, was observed by a panel of three experienced counselors (names), selected by the course instructor, as she conducted a counseling session. A rating form was used by the three judges to assess the counseling competence. A composite of these rating forms indicates that:

a. she showed genuine empathy in responses to client behavior.

b. she was able to help client to rationally analyze problems.

c. she helped client to formulate possible solutions to problems and helped client to evaluate these options.

d. client satisfaction was expressed.

Evaluation completed 7/28/71 and recorded on the transcript 8/1/71.

3. *Title of competence*

Knows the basic differences in sexual behavioral responses between human males and females.

Process by which competence was gained

Enrolled in and successfully completed the group learning opportunity in Human Sexual Response sponsored by MMSC and taught by .... The course involved readings, class discussions and a research paper.

Description of evidence of competence

Obtained a satisfactory score on the essay test constructed and scored by the instructor of the course. Was rated by the instructor to have achieved 85% of the instructional objectives of the course.

Evaluation completed 10/30/71 and recorded on the transcript 11/4/71.

Continued on next page

EXHIBIT 6

Continued from previous page

4. *Title of competence*

Knows the structure and function of the various types of correctional institutions in the U.S.A.

Process by which competence was gained

Enrolled in and successfully completed the group learning opportunity in Penal Systems sponsored by MMSC and taught by .... The course involved readings, class discussions, field trips and a research paper.

Description of evidence of competence

Obtained a satisfactory score on the objective test constructed by the instructor of the course. Was ranked by the instructor as being third in a class of twelve in terms of over-all performance in the elements of the process described above.

Evaluation completed 12/30/71 and recorded on the transcript 1/6/72.

5. *Title of competence*

Knows basic procedures used in correctional institutions.

Process by which competence was gained

Completed readings drawn from a list jointly compiled with Warden .... of the Shakopee Reformatory for Women. Student conducted interviews of six staff personnel, two guards and three inmates. Once a week, student met with Warden .... to discuss readings and content of interviews.

Description of evidence of competence

According to a general outline not given to the student in advance, the Warden and one other staff member (name) asked questions and requested elaborations and clarifications when appropriate. The two evaluators judged that the student had a thorough knowledge of all the basic correctional procedures.

Evaluation completed 3/29/72 and recorded on the transcript 4/6/72.

6. *Title of competence*

Knows, can apply and evaluate knowledge of the operation of a halfway house for women exoffenders.

Process by which competence was gained

Worked as a volunteer staff member at PI House for a three-

Continued on next page

EXHIBIT 6

Continued from previous page

month period. Was responsible for helping women adjust to release from corrections institution via group counseling sessions, job placement, and referral to appropriate community agencies. Worked alongside regular staff and helped put together resource referral directory appropriate to needs of women on parole.

Description of evidence of competence

Was observed by the Staff Coordinator, one staff member in referral work, and one of the women on parole (names).

Summary evaluation:

a. adjusted quickly to working as member of PI House team and demonstrated ability to work with women at the house.

b. coordinated the creation of a referral handbook with agencies to which the staff at PI House make regular referrals.

c. demonstrated understanding of the referral process and those agencies appropriate to PI House functions, that is, Ramsey County Welfare, food stamps, vocational training, job placement, and so on.

d. understands the procedures of PI House and its role as a halfway house for women parolees and as a diversionary service for women in trouble.

Evaluation completed 12/30/72 and recorded on the transcript 1/5/73.

7. *Title of competence*

Knows, can apply and evaluate knowledge of the role and function of a caseworker within a women's reformatory.

Process by which competence was gained

Served as an intern at Shakopee Reformatory for a three-month period working three days a week, including a one-month period observing procedures for intake, work assignments, group counseling sessions, parole and release procedures. Read various state policy and procedure manuals from Minnesota Department of Corrections. Served two months as a casework aide working with a full-time caseworker and on special assignment to two women inmates.

Continued on next page

EXHIBIT 6

Continued from previous page

Description of evidence of competence

Was observed by the Supervisor of Casework (name) and one of the caseworkers and the Director of Education (name) in the performance of various functions:

a. relates well with staff in staff meetings and demonstrates knowledge of various roles caseworker plays—coach, parent, authority figure, etc.

b. demonstrates basic understanding of various functions performed by caseworker in institutional setting of Minnesota Department of Corrections including education and rehabilitation.

c. establishes rapport with women inmates of lower socioeconomic status than her own.

d. demonstrates basic awareness of policies and procedures of Shakopee Womens Reformatory and its relationship to Minnesota Department of Corrections.

Evaluation completed 3/26/73 and recorded on the transcript 3/30/73.

While it does contain a record of course work completed at MMSC, it also narrates how Minerva achieved the competences she had set out to achieve. The narrative transcript is *the* logical record of the learner-as-central educational program. Its acceptance in the higher education community is essential if nontraditional programs are to reflect accurately what the student has achieved. The resistance to accepting this type of transcript is truly paradoxical. Though it does not show a gradepoint average, it does demonstrate what a student has learned and how. While it does not rank students and measure them one against the other, it does indicate how much (or how little) an individual has grown through the learning experience. The narrative transcript not only reveals how much, but provides an identifiable learning content. Its usefulness, therefore, should be great. Its value lies in showing where an individual is and how he/she got there. It might be somewhat cumbersome to handle, somewhat long to read, somewhat difficult to computerize. However, the quality of information the narrative transcript can generate makes it a much more valuable instrument than the standard transcript.

Counseling

Once students have had a chance to read the introductory material sent to them regarding crediting prior learning, they want to see someone who can tell them whether their experiences are worth considering for academic credit. At that point a counselor should be available to help them think through the many questions which invariably arise. All faculty, students, counselors, and administrators interviewed for this study agree on one thing: the process is too new and complex for students to be left completely on their own to prepare their documentation. Those students who had to do just that are convinced that they would have made a better showing if they had had help.

No matter how explicit the written material, it cannot cover all situations, nor can it allay the anxieties raised. Counseling, therefore, is crucial to success for a number of reasons. An accurate description of what is available to the student not only through the assessment of prior learning but through the total educational program helps everyone. The student is helped because he/she is better able to identify goals and ways to reach them. The faculty are helped because, regardless of their roles, they receive a student who is able to articulate needs, wants, and past accomplishments. The entire program or institution benefits because misunderstandings are kept at a minimum.

Counseling is a widely used, often misused, term. The skills needed in the initial phases of crediting prior learning are neither those of therapy nor those of academic advising. A nondirective "therapizing" approach to people who are looking for direction and answers is most inappropriate even though the counselor might be called upon to help a student work through some natural anxieties about the process. Just as inappropriate at this stage is the academic advising approach, which tends to be too narrow and oriented toward an academic discipline. What many students say they want and need at the beginning is someone who is definitely on their side, a student advocate—not an academic discipline advocate. Most students who apply for prior learning assessment have little idea of how to present their experiences in an academically acceptable fashion. The translation of life/work experiences into abstracted learning experiences is difficult enough. The task is even more difficult when those learning experiences must be clearly articulated or analyzed and synthesized.

In the early stages of crediting prior learning, the terms *counselor* and *counseling* are used to describe a function rather than a person. This distinction is especially important when dealing with a variety of programs and institutions. For example, there is a fundamental difference between the counseling function in a college whose faculty is responsible for assisting the student with the entire educational program and that function in a program which uses faculty only to assess prior learning. Institutions which employ the learner-as-central concept and whose faculty members guide individual students through the whole program usually ask a faculty person to counsel a student from beginning to end. In those schools where faculty only evaluate prior learning, the counseling function is frequently assigned to a professional counselor. In the latter instance a counselor is usually available to the student throughout his/her entire educational program, though it may not be the same person who assisted in the early phases of assessing prior learning. In these situations the counselors usually are part of a counseling office serving a large body of students, not just the special program that assesses prior learning. Between these two models are programs whose faculty have a varying degree of responsibility and whose counselor function varies accordingly.

A few institutions do not employ counselors and do not assign this function to faculty. They believe that adult students should have the maturity to understand the written material and translate experiences into an academically acceptable format. These schools tend to be those with less than a year's experience with assessing prior learning. A number of institutions which began with this notion have since added the counseling function. It bears repeating that the assessment of prior learning is too new and too complex to expect students to be able to prepare adequately by themselves. Maturity, per se, has little to do with it. If they lack something, it is sophistication in dealing with the concept and what is required, not maturity.

The counselor's role in the initial phase of evaluation should be that of a student advocate. The translation of experiences into an academically acceptable format, helping students to be confident and comfortable with the expression of these experiences, and, therefore, helping the student to meet the faculty advisor and his/her discipline on more equitable terms require an attitude and set of behaviors that are clearly pro student. These are necessary whether the function is carried out by a professional counselor or faculty member. Many students, especially adults returning to school after an absence of from ten to twenty years, not only are confused, but also have a tendency to underestimate the value of certain experiences. Counselors agree that this is true, especially for women who have not been involved in any significant "gainful employment." Both women and men who have significant paid work experience tend to be much more confident of their "worth" in the academic marketplace.

The following situation is presented to illustrate three points: (1) students need an advocate during the early stages of the process, (2) students need help in identifying the academically appropriate aspects of experience, and (3) some students are easily intimidated into believing that their experiences have no academic validity. The situation is real. The dialogue is a composite of several interviews arrived at through role playing.

Ms. M. is a thirty-five-year-old married woman, who lives with her husband and four preteen children in a comfortable suburban neighborhood. Before her marriage, Ms. M. finished approximately one year of college. In twelve years of marriage Ms. M. was forced to move four times because of her husband's work commitments. For the five years immediately preceding her application to a new special adult program, Ms. M. had attended another university as an evening student. Ms. M. attended school despite her husband's belittling remarks and rather hostile attitude. In spite of the fact that she had an excellent record (GPA of 3.6), Ms. M. was most insecure about what she knew and what she was capable of knowing.

In addition to attending school, for the past two years Ms. M. had been employed as a "lay" teacher in a preschool program for six severely disturbed children, ages three to seven. Ms. M. worked for two hours every morning under the supervision of a certified teacher who had a specialization in working with exceptional children. She was paid for her work and, as was learned later, referred to this as "my little job." Ms. M.'s educational goal was to earn her baccalaureate degree on the road toward a master's degree in special education so that she could qualify for certification to work with exceptional children. Her past formal educational efforts as well as her work experience were directly related to this goal and Ms. M. was attracted to the special adult program because it offered credit for prior learning. Since she already had 140 quarter credits of formal education behind her, it was important for Ms. M. to finish the baccalaureate program as soon as possible. Without access to the special adult program, the last "year" of the B.A. would have meant at least two and a half calendar years at the rate she was able to take formal course work.

Ms. M. was enrolled in a course in behavior modification the semester the special adult program began. After the first two weeks of the quarter it became apparent to the instructor that Ms. M. knew and could relate the majority of the content of the course. During the third week of the class, the instructor, Prof. H., asked Ms. M. to remain a few minutes after class to discuss her progress. During this conversation Prof. H. learned of Ms. M.'s work experience and the two spoke at some length about the behavior modification theories and techniques Ms. M. was employing in the work situation. Prof. H., who also happened to be an advisor to the special adult program, told Ms. M. about the program and Ms. M. made an appointment with one of the counselors in the special adult program. Dr. J. welcomed Ms. M. and asked her to be seated.

Dr. J: Prof H. tells me that you are in her Behavior Mod class and that you are quite a whiz!

Ms. M: That's very kind of her. Yes, I do know a little bit about behavior mod since I have to use it in my job.

Dr. J: Before we get into the details of your job, would you like me to tell you a little about how credit for experience works in this program?

Ms. M: Yes, that would be extremely helpful. I can't believe that I am going to get college credit just because I've lived.

Dr. J: You're right. You're *not* going to get credit just because you have lived but you will get credit for some of the college-level learning you have acquired through your life and work situations. In your case, it looks as though most of that credit, if not all, will come via your job since you are so far along and since your current objectives are directly in line with what you are doing.

Ms. M: Yes, I love my job, and I know this is silly, but I would love to have my own school someday. For that I'll need a master's degree in special ed.

Dr. J: I don't think that's silly at all.

Ms. M: That's good. Now, how do I get credit?

Dr. J: O.K. During this interview you and I will go over your work experience in some detail. Then you will write about your experiences, identifying what learning *you* think has taken place and in what areas. The material is reviewed by faculty in those areas and they make the determination of how many credits and in what areas. We will also ask your supervisor to send a corroborating statement. When everything is decided you are notified and if you have any problems with the decisions you have the right to appeal. Do you have any questions about this?

Ms. M: No—not at the moment.

Dr. J: O.K., so tell me about your job—oh, by the way, would you mind if we taped the rest of this interview? I've found that it's helpful for the students to take the tape and play it back at the time they do their portfolios.

Ms. M: No, I don't mind at all.

Dr. J: Now, tell me about your job.

Ms. M: Well, I work as a lay teacher for two hours each morning in a preschool situation designed for six children. All these children are severely emotionally disturbed, retarded, perceptually impaired, and all are functioning at a retarded level.

Dr. J: It must be difficult and wearing to work with children like that. How many of you are there?

Ms. M: Well, the head teacher—she runs the program, she has a master's in special education and is certified to work with exceptional children—and I are always there. Then there are always some volunteers who help out and we have at least one graduate student from this university every quarter.

Dr. J: Does the head teacher supervise all of you?

Ms. M: Oh, no. That would be almost impossible. She supervises me and one other person. I have the responsibility of supervising the others. On any one particular day there are about four or five of us there and Jane takes responsibility for me and one other person while I am responsible for the others.

Dr. J: So, you not only have responsibility for some of the children but you also have responsibility for volunteers and graduate students?

Ms. M: That's right.

Dr. J: How old are the children?

Ms. M: From three to seven.

Dr. J: And exactly how do you know what is wrong with each one? What I mean is, from the little I know about children of that age, and, believe me it is very little, isn't it difficult to get a definite diagnosis at that age?

Ms. M: It certainly is. We usually have some diagnosis

from the referring source, either a medical doctor or a psychiatrist, and if we feel that this information is not enough we use a child psychiatrist as a consultant. But even then, especially with the younger ones, all you really know is what you are able to observe. For example, a child who is subject to sudden severe temper tantrums could have brain damage, could have a severe emotional problem caused by nonorganic damage, or could have the kind of "problem" which disappears after a certain length of time just as suddenly as it began. There really isn't much definitive treatment available since the causes are often vague. We try to work primarily with their behavior since that, in some cases, *does* seem to be treatable and since that causes the child and those around him the most difficulty.

Dr. J: I see. Perhaps I could get a complete picture of what you do if you do this: pick a typical day and tell me what you do from the moment you get there until the moment you leave.

Ms. M: Well, I'll try. No day is really typical because something unforeseen always seems to happen. But we do have a routine. When the children first arrive we greet them and there follows a period of free play. Then . . .

Dr. J: Pardon me for interrupting, but before you go on, what do you mean by "greeting" them?

Ms. M: Well, from the time the child steps through the door we begin using the behavior modification technique of competing responses. We try to put desired responses in place of the undesired responses by rewarding the former and ignoring or punishing the latter. For example, eye contact and positive touching are encouraged and rewarded with praise and affection while undesirable aggressive or destructive behavior toward teachers, other children, or inanimate objects is ignored as much as possible. If the undesirable behavior becomes too severe, the child is punished, usually by removal from the play area.

Dr. J: I see, very interesting. Go on.

Ms. M: After the free play period there is usually a period when we work with children, one to one. During these times we work with the individual child on such things as picture recognition, manual dexterity skills or, if the child is autistic, we work just on establishing eye contact. Usually we use the techniques of concrete positive reinforcement on a continuous schedule and the shaping techniques of rewarding successive approximations of desired behavior.

Dr. J: You are beginning to lose me. I take it that what you are talking about are specific behavior modification techniques for which you understand both the theory and its application.

Ms. M: Oh, yes. You see, I've never had a behavior mod course. I am enrolled in the one taught by Professor H. After the first two weeks of the quarter she told me I didn't need to come to class anymore; that I could come in and take the final exam. I've learned a good deal about behavior mod from Jane and have also read some on my own.

Dr. J: That's fine. You don't have to go into details here with me. You can do that when you speak to the faculty advisor in that particular discipline. What is important is that *you* recognize what you've learned.

Ms. M: Well, it's all part of the job and I wouldn't be able to work with these children, the volunteers and graduate students, and the parents unless I understood what it was all about.

Dr. J: True. You said that you worked with the parents —well, that may be getting ahead of ourselves. Why don't you go on with your description of the day.

Ms. M: Yes, working with all the concerned adults— volunteers, graduate students, and parents—is a big part of the job. For example, my supervision of the volunteers and graduate students requires me to explain the needs of each child and to demonstrate the materials used as well as behavior mod techniques. I also have to be aware of the interaction between the volunteer or student and the child.

Dr. J: Do you find that sometimes you have to modify the behavior of the adults as well as the children?

Ms. M: Yes, I guess you could say that. We screen our volunteers and graduate students very carefully during the first two weeks. If there are major interpersonal or intrapersonal problems we have to counsel the volunteer or student out. This gets to be sticky, at times, but we feel it has to be done for the sake of the children. For instance, some of the volunteers just cannot bring themselves to punish a child who is exhibiting negative behavior. This really destroys an important part of the behavior mod program.

Dr. J: I can see where this would get to be sticky. Please go on.

Ms. M: During the refreshment period—juice and cookies —with all children sitting together, we again use the technique of competing responses. This usually is the only time that all the children are together in a structured activity and it gives us an opportunity to observe their behavior in a forced group situation. After the refreshment period, I often take one child at a time for a short period to a regular four-year-old normal preschool situation located in the same building. When appropriate social interaction with normal children occurs, it is encouraged and rewarded with social reinforcement and, again, the approximation of desired behaviors is rewarded.

Dr. J: I think you're getting a little too technical for *me,* again. But that's OK. I don't have to understand it all so long as you are able to articulate it.

Ms. M: Well, that about ends the two-hour day.

Dr. J: A while back you mentioned that you also worked with parents. When does that happen?

Ms. M: Oh, yes. Well, sometimes when they pick the children up, sometimes later on in the day on the telephone, or later on in person.

Dr. J: What do you mean when you say you work with the parents?

Ms. M: It depends on the situation. I spend a lot of time talking about the child's progress. In many instances, much time is also spent in trying to help them accept the fact that their child is "exceptional" and will probably need special schooling or care indefinitely. In other cases, I try to convince parents that though the child is handicapped, there are strengths and potential competences that can be developed. I also act as a referral source by discussing with the parents the possible programs or further training available to the child as he grows older.

Dr. J: I would imagine that working with these parents presents many problems. What is the most common problem?

Ms. M: I would say—guilt. The enormous guilt feelings associated with having an exceptional child are the biggest problem for parents. First of all, they find it difficult to accept some of our methods because they perceive that we punish a child for what he *is* rather than what he *does*. Unless this is worked through, the parents will not continue the behavior mod program at home. Secondly, the guilt gets in the way of their relationships with each other and with the child's brothers and sisters.

Dr. J: I would have guessed that guilt was the biggest problem. Well, Ms. M., I think that I have gotten a pretty good picture of the job and what you seem to have learned from it. Let me just summarize for a minute. From what you have said, your learning seems to be in four areas: (1) an understanding of the exceptional child, (2) theory and practice of behavior modification techniques, (3) supervision of graduate students and volunteers, and (4) the counseling of parents. I will see

to it that you get to the appropriate faculty advisors to have this learning evaluated. In the
meantime, here is an outline of how you might
write these up. It has some examples which should
help. I'll also give you this tape because I think
much of what we have spoken about will be helpful in preparing your narrative. If you don't have
a tape machine at home, feel free to use one of
ours. Are there any questions you have at this
time?

Ms. M: No, I don't think so, but I'm sure I'll have some as
soon as I leave. May I call you if I do have questions?

Dr. J: Of course, and I hope this has been helpful.

Ms. M: Thank you so much. Yes, it's been extremely helpful. Talking about all I do with you has made me
realize that I know an awful lot more than I
thought I did. I've never felt that way just thinking about my job.

Dr. J: I'm glad it has been helpful. I really enjoyed talking with you, and remember, if you have any
questions, please call. If not, just prepare the narrative, get the letter of reference from Jane, and
we will contact you about appointments when
we've had a chance to look the material over.

Ms. M: Thanks so much and—goodbye now.

Dr. J: Goodbye.

Ms. M. entered the special adult program the following quarter and was awarded twenty-five quarter hours' credit
for the learning achieved through her work experience. The
credits were awarded on the basis of the narrative Ms. M. wrote,
the letter from her supervisor, and an oral examination by a
faculty team representing special education, supervision, and
counseling. Dr. J. saw her twice more to help her prepare the
narrative, especially to help her articulate and be comfortable
with what she had learned. Ms. M. took only one course, student teaching, to complete her degree. Since the School of Education had been familiar with her work because they used the
setting as a student-teacher placement for graduate students,

she was allowed to do her "student teaching" there, with Jane as her supervisor. After completing her B.A., Ms. M. went on to finish her master's degree and is currently establishing her own preschool for disturbed children.

Dr. J.'s manner, the questions he asked, and the comments he made clearly demonstrate a student-advocate position. Nothing was promised but he did convey the message that Ms. M. had quite a number of skills and learning events which were worthy of being considered for credit. Ms. M. was made comfortable enough with what she had accomplished to be able to articulate her learning and skills quite adequately. The use of the tape recorder in these initial sessions is extremely helpful. For many students this is their first experience in identifying, ordering, and abstracting the learning derived from experience. If a narrative is demanded of the student, the material from the initial counseling session can prove an invaluable base to build on.

The observation made by Ms. M. that talking about her experiences to Dr. J. had helped her to see the knowledge base of her experience is important to note. First of all, most of the people with whom Ms. M. had spoken to regarding her job either did not understand what she was really doing or belittled it. The perspective received by just thinking about experience is never as clear and organized as when one is asked to write about it or systematically discuss it with someone who is trained to listen. Dr. J.'s only agenda was helping Ms. M. clarify and articulate her experiences.

Imagine that Ms. M. had her first encounter with someone who had his own agenda, someone not particularly sympathetic to the process, and someone who had been assigned by his chairperson to represent the interest of the department in this new venture. The interview might have gone something like this:

> Prof. F: Well, sit down, little lady, and let me take just a few moments to read over your application. Hmmm . . . I see you have accumulated about a hundred and forty quarter hours of credit. I

also see that some of these are more than ten years old and they might not be credited—at least they wouldn't be credited in the regular program. I'm not sure what the people in this program have negotiated with the higher-ups . . . (a pause) . . . Now, let's see, you haven't had much work experience, have you?

Ms. M: Well, I've . . .

Prof. F: Let me interject something here. In order for you to receive any credit for your work experience you are going to have to show us that a *substantial* and *significant* amount of learning has taken place as a result of that experience . . .

Ms. M: I understand that I . . .

Prof. F: You know, we are not giving away credits here just because you have lived! For instance, don't expect any credit for having had babies. We discussed all that at a recent meeting and decided that being a mother was O.K., but it's not college-level work . . . (laughter).

Ms. M: I wasn't expecting credit for that. I was hoping . . .

Prof. F: And the secretarial work you did before you were married probably won't count either.

Ms. M: I didn't think it would but . . .

Prof. F: Let's see, your latest work was as a "lay" teacher —never did like that terminology; it sounds dirty (Prof. F. gives Ms. M. a significant sneer). So, you worked with severely disturbed children. You know that I am a psychologist. . . . No? How could you have known. Well, I am, and I'm a full professor, which means that I've been around a long time. I'm not telling you this to impress you, I just want you to know that if you expect credit for this work you are going to have to show me, or someone from another discipline, that you really know your stuff. (almost as an aside) . . . . I wonder how they let you work with disturbed children when you have had no proper training. . . . Just exactly what kind of a place is this?

Ms. M: It's a privately operated preschool for six children, ages three to seven, who have different kinds of problems.

Prof. F: What kinds of problems?

Ms. M: Some are retarded, some have impaired perception, some are autistic . . .

Prof. F: These are serious cases. What kind of controls or supervision do you have?

Ms. M: You mean me or the program?

Prof. F: Well, both.

Ms. M: The woman who runs the school has a master's degree in special education and is certified to work with exceptional children. She supervises me. We use psychiatrists and other physicians for diagnostic and supervisory help.

Prof. F: What, no psychologists?

Ms. M: No, not at this time.

Prof. F: Well, let's see, what do you think you could get credit for here?

Ms. M: I really don't know. I was hoping you would help me with that.

Prof. F: Well, Mrs. M., from what you have written here it looks like you are involved mostly with such things as, and I quote from your application, "seeing that the children do not hurt each other . . . serving juice and cookies . . . accompanying children to the regular nursery school program." All these sound like tasks of maintenance and do not seem to be creditable in our university.

Ms. M: You don't think that I can get credit for any of this?

Prof. F: No, Mrs. M., I frankly do not. You see, as I told you before, we give credit only for meaningful learning experiences, and these do not seem to fall in that category. I would suggest that you enter our regular program in special education and get the proper training for what you're doing. After all, we *do* have to see to it that people are properly trained. This is our responsibility to those children and their parents. Thanks for coming in and good luck.

Ms. M: (somewhat stunned and visibly dejected) Thank you, sir, for taking the time to speak with me.

This interview would have made Ms. M. quite insecure about what she knew and, indeed, even more insecure about her job. It is quite obvious that Prof. F. had his own agenda and was more interested in that than in finding out exactly what it was that Ms. M. knew. What Ms. M. wrote on her application was rather sketchy and somewhat conservatively stated. It was apparent from the written description that Ms. M. saw herself somewhat more as a maintenance person than as a professional. While the supervising teacher had tried to help Ms. M. interpret her role more in line with what Ms. M. actually knew and did, consulting psychiatrists, social workers, and other professionals tended to treat her as a nonprofessional.

One of the problems in assessing prior learning is that many students tend to measure themselves rather than what they know by how many credits they receive. Like the parents of Ms. M.'s exceptional children, they tend to confuse the punishment of behavior with the punishment of the child. As one counselor put it, "There is such a personal investment in these portfolios—in people describing very sensitive areas of their lives—that they tend to see their whole worth as a person wrapped up in how many credits they receive." The initial counseling, subsequent counseling, and any help given during the time of portfolio preparation must constantly stress that the assessment of prior learning means exactly that, judgments about learning and not about how students have lived their lives.

Awareness of the sensitivities involved must exist at the first contact. It is possible to derive creditable learning from extremely personal experiences but to do so the counselor must understand that what is being dealt with *is* creditable learning and not problems which require therapy. The latter might be present but must not be confused with the former.

Prior Learning Assessment Seminars

As a sequel to or in place of initial individual counseling sessions, some programs have established some form of credit seminar devoted to helping students further think through experiences in academically acceptable terms. Ultimately designed to help students prepare their portfolios, these seminars also allow them to share experiences and begin the process of analyzing each other's learning dimensions as well as their own. Depending on how the program handles the counseling function, these seminars are led either by faculty advisors or counselors. Their duration is never more than one semester, and in at least one place the seminar is designed as a three-week module. Although the credits given for these seminars vary from one to four, the seminars *are* being credited as learning experiences. Students learn how to translate their experiences into academically communicable form. Depending on the structure of the seminars, students can come away with heightened self-awareness, interpersonal skills, and confidence in their abilities. Many counselors and faculty indicate that the entire process of assessing prior learning is one of the most significant learning experiences students can have.

In one program the preparation of portfolios came as an unexpected benefit from two courses designed especially to have people share, in small groups, their life/work experiences. The director of the New Resources Program at the College of New Rochelle describes the situation as follows: "We have a lot of people doing portfolios now because they took the time to take two life-experience credit workshops. We didn't set them up as direct training for portfolio preparation. The portfolio is one person's attempt to get credit; the life-experience workshop is a community of learning for adults. Each workshop has a different focus: one is focused on the person, the other on the community. The academic slant is to try to get the student to analyze his or her experience from a personal social interaction standpoint and to get the student to do the same for personal interaction in coming to terms with the community. The groups are small, ten to fifteen. They are not encounter groups or rap sessions even though a lot of personal stuff is dealt with. We've found that as the program progresses, the best portfolios come from people who have attended the workshops." The program now encourages students to take these life-experience workshops both for their intrinsic value and because the workshops will help them prepare the portfolio.

One of the most often heard criticisms of the narrative as a mechanism to demonstrate learning is that it relies solely on the ability to communicate what has been learned in writing. If the ability to communicate in writing what has been learned is central, then the prior learning assessment seminar can fulfill a double function. The seminar can work with the skills necessary to translate experience into learning and can help the student develop the writing abilities needed to describe the learning in that manner.

Evergreen State College's guidelines for "external [prior learning] credit" state that:

> Credit should not be given for experience or skills in themselves, but rather for *demonstrating understanding:* conscious, conceptual, verbal understanding. Operationally, this means *explaining* and *communicating* what the person knows so that someone else who doesn't understand it can do so. . . . And when someone's experience, skills, or knowledge is put in the form of conscious verbal understanding—an extended paper or report—then it becomes feasible for a committee to make a fair decision about how much college credit to give. . . . We realize, however, that this procedure is a disadvantage to people who deserve external credit because they know a lot, but who have been alienated from all school and school-like activities. We feel we have developed a module that will help such people get the credit they deserve.

The module referred to here is specifically geared to helping people learn how to express themselves in writing.

Prior learning assessment seminars have much to offer students, faculty, and administrators. As refined counseling tools, the seminars help students to prepare better portfolios and give them further confidence in communicating their learning. Faculty receive narratives which are much more refined and students who are much more articulate about what they know. Finally, many more students can be handled in a group than individually. Since these are credit-bearing seminars, they produce revenue through tuition or through student credit hours in an FTE-formula system. This last point is important because this method can go a long way toward offsetting the cost of preparing students for the evaluation of prior learning. While this particular revenue would not compensate for faculty advisor time in all situations, it does partially pay for the counseling time needed. The revenue would pay for some of the faculty advisor time in those programs which use the faculty advisor as counselor.

Chapter IV

ﾒﾒﾒﾑﾑﾑ

Documentation

The next step in the process is to assemble in some acceptable form the material to be assessed. Such a form could include documentation by transfer credit, by standard examination results, by a third party, by product assessment, by student narrative, and by the new Continuing Education Unit (CEU), although the latter poses some difficult problems. The entire package, involving any or all of these elements presented for assessment, is called the student's portfolio. (In some programs *portfolio* refers to the narrative written by the student, but this discussion uses *portfolio* to designate the total package of which the narrative is one part.)

What is to be assembled, of course, depends directly on what is to be credited. If it is the experience itself, then acceptable proof that the experience has taken place is required. If it is learning derived from the experience, then proof of the learning is necessary. If the learning must be demonstrated at a particular level of abstraction, then the proof, or documentation, must reflect that level.

For example, obtaining the rank of sergeant on an urban police force is a measureable achievement, but does not demonstrate learning, in and of itself. It can be argued that a base line of minimum learning is necessary to reach this rank. Certain tests had to be taken, certain leadership qualities had to be acquired which demand some learning, and specific knowledge of the internal workings of the police department and how the department relates to the larger community is assumed. It can be argued further that the closer this particular position is to the educational goal, the less direct examination of learning need take place. If the sergeant is applying to a specialized baccalaureate program in Police Science, the mere fact of the attained rank could be enough to grant a certain number of credits. In this situation there is a common, often unstated, measure of agreement between the consumer (the police department) and the educational program as to what constitutes desired results. If the police sergeant enters a liberal arts program, however, these common elements are not present. The rank itself loses some intrinsic value because the base line of minimum knowledge required to achieve it becomes less clear. If the program is learning-centered, the sergeant will have to articulate his/her learning to fulfill the desired outcomes of that particular liberal arts curriculum.

Every life/work experience carries with it the assumption of minimal learning. Some learning will be creditable toward a college degree, some will not. The decision about credit needs to be made before the process begins. The documentation of that learning which is creditable then becomes focused, and at least some of the irrelevant material is eliminated. It has been argued that too narrow a focus limits the documentation and often bypasses certain learnings which could have been creditable. On the other hand, wide limits and loosely defined criteria are apt to elicit a mountain of material for faculty to sift through. Most programs report that they usually get what they ask for. If all that is creditable, for example, is the exact material covered in particular courses, then all the student need do is demonstrate that knowledge by whatever means are normally employed. The student whose knowledge surpasses that required by the course or the student whose knowledge is similar to, but not just the same as, the content of the course can get credit only for that part of the learning which corresponds to the course content. It stands to reason, therefore, that documentation will reflect the narrow focus and some knowledge *will* be bypassed. The program has to decide whether this loss is too high a price for having easy-to-manage, narrow limits.

Transfer Credit

Strictly speaking, the transfer of credit is not an integral part of this work because it deals with prior *academic* credentialing rather than with crediting prior learning as defined in Chapter 1. However, I include it because it is *the* universally accepted method for granting students advanced standing or waiving future course requirements. Furthermore, transfer credit is so much a part of the higher education establishment that one can hardly envisage a system of rewards which omitted it. A student transferring from College X to College Y has the previous academic work credited, usually as part of the admission process and usually by someone in the office of admissions or the office of the registrar.

Only in unusual instances does a faculty member get involved in this process and then it might go something like this: "Hmmm. . . . let me see, you took English 404 and received a 'B.' English 404 looks very much like our Humanities 418. Who did you say your professor was? Oh, what do you know about that! He and I did our undergraduate work at the same school. Now, you said you brought in the outline for the course. Let's see. Ah. . . . hmmm. . . . Yes, you seem to have covered just about what we cover. No. . . . I don't believe I need to read the paper you did for the course, although the title, 'Alliterative References Found in *Hamlet* and *The Happy Hooker*,' does intrigue me. Let's see, we shall give you credit for Humanities 418 which leaves you free to take one more elective."

The assumptions underlying the transfer of credits are that: (1) the contents of the two courses are identical or nearly identical; (2) the level of instruction is comparable; (3) the student learned in the first college that which would be expected to be learned in the second college at a level of "B"; (4) there is no loss of knowledge for seven to ten years after the course was taken at the first college, but after the agreed upon number of years has lapsed there is complete loss of knowledge. As questionable as these assumptions may be, they are rarely tested. At best, the transfer process attempts to equate levels of *instruction*. No attempt is made to examine whatever learning has gone on and how it has been built upon, changed, or stagnated. Yet this particular process is so deeply ingrained in the higher education establishment that every program or institution, regardless of how innovative they try to be, must use it.

In some cases, as in Florida, New York, and Minnesota, the transfer of credit is mandated by law for the public institutions. Thus a program such as the Florida External Degree Program and institutions such as Empire State College and Minnesota Metropolitan College must accept an associate degree at face value. This procedure, especially mandating at least half of a program of studies, causes problems to those institutions which view all previous learning—academic or not—in relation to a total program of studies. Serling, at Empire State College refers to the problem of "top down" versus "bottom up" assessment. To evaluate from the bottom up is to count the student's academic credits and see what their additive value is, whereas top-down assessment involves defining the student's degree program and then evaluating prior learning in terms of that program. Empire State College believes emphasis should be placed on what is needed to complete the program, not on how many months of credit have been collected. But "no matter how total the acceptance of the idea of 'top down,' we are still bound by SUNY [State University of New York] convention to give so-called junior status to the holder of an associate degree. Given these realities, we should be aware that some part of assessment will always remain 'bottom up' " (personal interview).

I do not recommend that the automatic recognition of previous academic credits be abandoned. Although such a step might be philosophically desirable and well in line with an educational system that is totally focused on learning, the abolition of transfer credits at this time is neither practical nor in the best interest of the student. Yet we should acknowledge that the current practice is far from perfect and needs to be viewed honestly for what it does and does not do. Despite their administrative convenience, transfer credits only show that students have been exposed to a certain body of knowledge and that they have achieved a letter grade which tells practically nothing of what has actually been learned and how that learning has helped them develop.

Standard Examinations

Unlike transfer credit, credit for passing various tests is most relevant to this book because it can apply to prior nonacademic learning. The exams taken might be standardized national tests such as the CLEP tests, the Advanced Placement Program tests, the USAFI Subject Standardized Test, or CEEB or ACT achievement tests. Or they might be constructed by the faculty of one department or institution for use only within that institution. Ruyle and Geiselman (Cross, Valley and Associates, 1974, pp. 59–60) indicate that although standardized examinations are being accepted more and more, the way their results are used is still a problem. "Some institutions accept the results only for placement or to waive required courses, while others grant extensive credit for them toward a degree. Credit by examination remains controversial in some institutions because of disagreements over which examinations to use, what scores are acceptable for credit, how much credit should be allowed, and whether credit will be accepted by another institution." Yet in spite of this controversy, credit by examination is widespread enough to have an impact on most institutions. "Considering both the standardized and institutional examinations together, fully 93 percent of colleges and universities report using one or another kind of test for granting credit or waiving course requirements: 70 percent of them employ *both* external and internal examinations; 19 percent use only *standardized exams;* 4 percent use only *institutional exams;* and 7 percent report *no* use of either type of test" (p. 65).

The correspondence I conducted for this book affirms Ruyle and Geiselman's findings. All institutions which submitted written guidelines on faculty-based models of granting credit for prior learning state that one or more of the national standardized testing programs are available to their students. In addition, slightly more than one hundred institutions that have no provision for faculty-based models also provide one of the national standardized programs and/or institutional examinations. As is true for transfer credits, some states now mandate that passing grades on CLEP tests or some other national exams be accepted by upper-division or four-year institutions for lower-division work. While this action indicates increasing acceptance of such testing, the problems created by legislative mandate are similar to those created by requiring recognition of the associate degree.

The extent to which standardized testing programs have become acceptable to administrators and legislators is encouraging. Faculty acceptance has been somewhat slower in coming. Many of the faculty I interviewed say they are reluctant to accept the national examination programs because they are usually not consulted about the way the tests are used. In most institutions the results of CLEP and other standardized examinations are handled by admission officers or registrars. In many instances faculty have (or feel they have) nothing to say about which scores are considered acceptable for waiver or for credit. These faculty do not resent the tests or what the tests are attempting to accomplish; they simply feel resigned to still another example of administrative fiat without faculty or faculty/ student input.

The other impact of standardized examinations is linked

to the basic issue of the meaning of the baccalaureate degree. There is rising concern that standardized tests perpetuate the curricular status quo, that they discourage curricular and instructional innovations, that many students—especially adults out of school for ten years or more—are not test-sophisticated, and that learning gained from independent, life/work experiences does not fall into neat "course equivalent" packages. Keeton identifies the issue as follows: "We have hailed the CLEP tests as a breakthrough toward enabling students to gain recognition for learning without doing it in regular college courses. The CLEP tests, however, are essentially abstractions from very traditional liberal arts and disciplinary objectives. If anything, their availability widens the service gap between those for whom those objectives are appropriate and those who need different kinds of postsecondary education" (Vermilye, 1972, p. 141).

Yet perhaps these testing programs are being criticized unfairly. After all, they do not claim to do any more than they actually do, and what they do with respectable reliability and validity is measure learning content in various areas of the curriculum. Further, faculty did and continue to have an input because the examinations are prepared by nationally recognized scholars in the various disciplines. It would also be a mistake to claim that *all* adult students are shy of the tests or are not test-sophisticated. Many students take advantage of the opportunity to receive credit by examination. Many more will continue to do so. Like transfer credit, credit by examination should be encouraged when *it is appropriate*. The gaining of credit through national standardized testing programs and/or institutional exams should be neither treated as a panacea nor totally rejected. Those programs and institutions dedicated to placing the student's learning at the center of the educational process will find credit by examination to be one of many useful methods to help plan the student's total program of studies.

Third-Party Validation

Any substantiation of an experience, or the learning gained from it, by someone or something outside the institution granting credit can be considered third-party validation or corroboration. The term *corroboration* is usually employed when the third-party data are used in addition to on-campus assessment; *validation* is used when third-party information is used in lieu of on-campus assessment. Third-party validation may come from such sources as certificates, licenses, transfer credits, standardized national test results, letters of reference, job descriptions, supervisors' evaluations, and evaluations by panels of outside experts. Although transfer credits are not seen usually as third-party data, they are included in this category because, technically, they are a form of third-party validation.

In the context of this book, third-party validation or corroboration is any information used to evaluate prior learning which has *not* been generated between students and faculty. In faculty-based models of assessing prior learning only student narratives and evaluation techniques which directly involve students and faculty are designated as "first- and second-party" validation.

What and how much shall be validated by third parties depends, again, on what is to be credited. In most programs, third-party data are an integral part of the documentation and any particular piece of such material must be just as relevant as what the student presents directly. Much irrelevant information can be avoided by early decisions about which particular items are appropriate and exactly what they should reveal.

It is unfair to the student and to the third party to request information in a vague, nonspecific manner. Many administrators and counselors indicate a high level of frustration because letters of reference from supervisors, for example, are not giving them what they want. In some instances, the student or supervisor is not informed of exactly what is desired. "Obtain a letter of reference from your supervisor" does not give any direction. But even when a letter does state that the validation should indicate what the student has learned from that experience, the reply is rarely specific enough to be useful to the faculty evaluating prior learning. For one thing, the community at large may not define learning in the same manner as does the educational program. For another, translating experience into learning is just as foreign to the larger community as it is to the student. In the long run, what needs to be sent out is a fairly detailed questionnaire which will get at the desired information in the manner to be useful to those doing the assessment.

The sample letter of the Long Island Learning Center, Empire State College (Exhibit 7), is a good example of an

---

EXHIBIT 7
GUIDE FOR THIRD-PARTY VERIFICATION LETTER

RE: Job Description and Letter of Reference for ....

Dear

An Empire State College student has asked you to write a verification letter. As you may know, students at Empire State College may earn credit toward degrees for prior learning gained through life experience. This experience may take a variety of forms: on-the-job training, in-house training programs, self-study programs, travel, independent reading, and so forth. To receive credit for such life learning experiences the student must first describe the learning they seek credit for and then verify that such learning has taken place. Verification takes a variety of forms: evaluation by scholars at the Learning Center or other institutions of higher learning, or evaluation by persons working in the field who have demonstrated competence in a particular area.

The letter which an Empire State College student has asked you to write is much more than a traditional letter of recommendation. This letter should:

1. Specify the period of time the student has worked in your field
2. Describe the particular duties the student was required to perform in your setting
3. Describe the learning involved in performing these tasks
4. Evaluate the level of the student's performance

Continued on next page

EXHIBIT 7

Continued from previous page

The letter is basically a job description requiring specific references to the knowledge and information needed to perform particular tasks. The letter should answer the following questions:

1. What are the "normal" requirements of the job?
2. What changes in responsibility has the student successfully mastered?
3. What growth or learning has the student shown?
4. How does the student's performance compare with that of other colleagues who hold bachelor's degrees?

Your letter is a difficult one to write and you may wish to ask the student to assist you by taking responsibility for preparing the information necessary to write the letter. Since the letter may be used as a basis for granting academic credit, the contents will be carefully scrutinized. If you have any questions about this letter or would like any further information, please call us at (516) 997-4700.

Sincerely yours,

---

attempt to ask the right questions. This letter is sent after the student requests a reference and goes a long way to tell the third party exactly what is wanted. At the very least, such a letter would stave off the following response received by another program on behalf of a woman who had worked a considerable time as a teacher aide: "To Whom it May Concern: Mrs. C. M. worked as a teacher aide at P. School for a period of three and one-half years from February 1969 to June 1971. C. is no doubt the most outstanding aide we have employed. She is very sensitive to individual children and very capable of handling small and large groups. We believe her success as an aide influenced her decision to pursue further education. We not only highly recommend her to others but would personally be interested in hiring her as a teacher when she is available." The letter was signed by the principal and the assistant principal. Nice letter. Typical letter. Excellent reference. But what does it really say? All the letter actually verifies is that Mrs. M. served successfully as a teacher aide for three and a half years. If the receiving educational institution has a close working relationship with this particular elementary school, knows and understands exactly what is expected of teacher aides, and understands from previous experience what these two validators mean by "outstanding," then it might have a base line from which to begin. Even so, the institution would not necessarily know what "being sensitive to individual children" means or, still more vague, being able to "handle small and large groups." Do they mean that Mrs. M. is an effective disciplinarian, that her children are always nice and quiet, that they walk single file without talking to the bathroom, and that Mrs. M. is always in control of the children's behavior?

It is difficult to judge exactly what this letter was supposed to convey. Personnel departments usually verify employment. The fact that this letter was signed by both the principal and the assistant principal and has a praiseworthy tone indicates that it was meant to do more than just verify employment. Were the two men aware that Mrs. M. was attempting to receive academic credit for her experience as an aide? If so, how and by whom was this fact conveyed? Like any other evaluation device, the third-party item needs to have as much reliability and validity as possible. Does it measure what is actually being credited? If so, how well does it perform that function?

The third party should be as familiar with the total educational program as possible. As an example, one institution works very closely with the Head Start program in that city. As a matter of fact, the special educational program which offers credit for prior learning was started because of the large number of Head Start employees who wanted further education toward a degree. During the first year of the program, the faculty attempted to work with the evaluation devices used for purposes of promotion within the Head Start program. These were supervisory evaluations which described some competences but failed to address the question of what was learned. The Head Start program was quite satisfied with the form and content of these evaluations since they served its purposes well. The educational program at first accepted these evaluations at face value because the college program had not thought through exactly what it was crediting.

As this question began to be clarified, the Head Start evaluations began to make the faculty more and more uncomfortable. Learning derived from the acquisition of skills and competences was emerging as that which was to be credited, not these achievements alone. By the beginning of the second year, the program decided to forego these evaluations altogether and rely solely on what the student could communicate. While the narrative of learning has a great deal of intrinsic value, the third-party corroboration could have been useful to the evaluators.

What was needed was for the educational program and the Head Start program to work together to devise an evaluation form which could serve both purposes. During the first year and a half of the educational program, no one worked with the Head Start program on anything other than procedural matters relating to tuition waivers, certain aspects of admissions, and physical facilities in which to hold classes. During the latter part of the second year, when the question of what was to be credited was answered along with some other basic questions of curriculum, the education director of the Head Start program and the curriculum liaison person from the educational program began to meet regularly. By the end of the second year, the new evaluation form had been devised and some other important interfaces had begun to develop.

It is not always possible to have this kind of direct contact with third parties. When possible, however, a relationship should be created early enough so that confusions are kept to a minimum and the benefits derived from the interface can be maximized.

Two questions raised frequently in relation to third-party data bear mentioning. First, how current does the validation need to be to be useful? The answer, of course, depends entirely on how any one particular program views the total educational plan. When the learner-as-central concept is associated with the philosophy that prior learning must be tied to future goals, only that learning which can be demonstrated in the present and which can be directly related to the future goal is creditable. In this model students must demonstrate learning directly and third parties can only corroborate it. Furthermore, only those data which corroborate what is *retained and demonstrated* are useful. If the program allows validation by third-party data, it assumes (1) that the data adequately reflect what the program needs to know in order to credit directly from that information and (2) that, unless otherwise specified, there is no statute of limitations on the data. What holds true for transfer credits holds true for any third-party verification which is *directly* creditable, be it a certificate, a license, or a letter of reference: in general, any corroboration which bears directly on what the student *knows or can demonstrate,* regardless of how old this item may be, is useful.

The second question is, How should self-growth experiences be substantiated? Some programs attempting to grant credit for learning which has taken place as a result of structured growth experiences feel more obligated to corroborate this learning by a third party than they do so-called straight intellectual learning. Student statements about what has been learned and how that learning is being applied do not seem to be sufficient when that learning bears a stated emotional content. All learning involves emotional as well as intellectual content and processes. However, learning through self-growth, encounter groups, sensitivity sessions, and psychotherapy is not as well accepted yet as learning derived from independent reading, for example.

This issue was discussed, at length, with one program director, who finally stated that it would be *political suicide* not to corroborate learning achieved through a psychotherapeutic group process. Everyone understood that learning could take place through independent reading but few believed, or could accept, the other. If the motivation for seeking substantiation of these learnings is political, fine! If the motivation is really to corroborate, why? Cannot the student's narrative of what has been learned through encounter groups be treated the same as verifications of all other learning? Does how the learning took place matter more than that it has occurred? The real problem is that criteria for this type of learning are not as clear as for others. Once these are clarified and accepted the problems should disappear.

Product Assessment

The product assessment, as a form of third-party verification, recognizes that a certain manufactured piece of work has intrinsic, creditable value. The most common examples are paintings, sculptures, pieces of music, and other works of art or craft. These products can be directly evaluated by a panel of experts from within or without the university and credited in the appropriate areas of the curriculum.

Student Narrative

All programs require some form of narrative statement from students, whether these be descriptions of experience, learning, or both. Below are examples of instructions from four institutions:

Edison College. "With the assistance of an Edison College advisor, the student then prepares a survey of the areas of knowledge to be assessed and organizes the documentation, if any, that supports the application. The primary purpose of the survey and documentation is to focus attention on the college-level knowledge or skill claimed by the student. Any information which will be helpful in identifying and evaluating this knowledge should be included. Each survey will be unique; therefore, the material presented should include a clear and detailed statement of the college-level knowledge claimed. It may also include, where applicable, such documentation as the following: a listing of formal or informal educational activities;

work experience, with a description of duties which have been instrumental in the acquisition of the knowledge claimed, and the evaluation of supervisors when appropriate; and a portfolio of works such as reports, published books or articles, speeches, works of art."

Goddard College. "A personal essay in four parts. (This is the most important part of the petition.)

"A. In the first part of it you should list, one by one, the experiences included in the petition, tell how long you were involved in them, how much time per week you put in, where they took place, when, and who your principal associates in the experience were. For example, I'll list two fictitious experiences of the sort that might be included in a petition.

> Assistant dance instructor for five years, spent approximately five hours per week. At the Allen Academy of Dance, Cleveland, Ohio, from 1953 to 1958. William Allen, director of the academy, was my principal supervisor. I also worked with Martha Rubenstein, who was his associate.
>
> Administrative assistant at a hydraulics research laboratory, for six years, forty hours per week. U.S. Geological Survey Laboratories, Denver, Colorado, from 1962 to 1968. Emma Willard, hydraulics engineer was my immediate supervisor.

"B. After you have listed the experiences, tell in a separate paragraph exactly how much you think each experience should accelerate you, and how much you think the total should come to. For example, using the instances above, 'I believe my work at the Allen Academy is worth at least one semester's advancement, and my work at the hydraulics laboratory is worth another one. I entered the program with six semesters to complete. Since I am now working on my second semester, I hope with this petition I can graduate after completing two additional semesters.'

"C. Then go on to a detailed narrative of your experiences, explaining just what you did, how much of it was routine, how much involved original work on your part. At this point you should refer to the letters and other documentation which you include in the petition. Tell how you now feel about the experience, what parts of it you regard as being of greatest educational value, and make a careful description of exactly what you learned.

"D. The final portion of your essay should be a section explaining how what you learned through the experiences fits in with your present educational plans, what carry-overs there were, how the experiential learning continues to be of service to you. Be certain to go over the whole essay process carefully with your advisor. When it is completed, put it in a binder labeled 'Essay,' and don't put anything else in that binder."

Loretto Heights College. "What is the Process for Proposing for Credit? A. Meet with a UWW Advisor and Coordinator of Documentation and Research to discuss past experiences. B. On basis of (A), develop proposal draft which incorporates the following information: (1) title of experience; (2) where, when, how much time; (3) who worked with or supervised by names and titles; (4) specific skills/competences learned, further developed; (5) general knowledge/awareness gained and how does this experience relate to where you are now?"

University of Massachusetts. "Step One (to be completed by the student)—building a portfolio describing the past experience in order to develop a rationale for crediting that experience.

"A. *An Inclusive Vita* is to be completed giving a chronological history of the past experience. Each entry includes a detailed description of the job or experience including titles, responsibilities, skills, competencies, knowledges, training, etc.

"B. *Thematic Vita.* After completing a chronological vita and examining all entries included, themes are derived from the past experiences. For example, this may mean that the student had two jobs, one in a travel agency and one working in a day care center, and that both were important in developing his/her skills in human relations. One theme or interest area might then be Human Relations. By referring back to the completed chronological vita, the student describes aspects of the experience in the travel agency and day care center which added knowledge or helped develop skills in human relations.

The end product is a thematic vita describing the past experience by area of interest or expertise, emphasizing the competence or knowledge gained.

"C. *Documentation* such as letters of reference, proposals, evaluations, articles, books, tapes, personnel folders, etc., supplements the vita material."

These examples are representative and, as can be seen, some are more explicit than others. Some institutions, such as Goddard College, clearly value the narrative part of the portfolio above all others. The foundation of all narratives is the capacity to communicate experience and learning *in writing*. There are many and varied levels of competence and learning to be sorted out of the narrative for purposes of assessment. The prime requisite, however, is that the student be able to state his/her case by means of the written word. One need not apologize for this requirement. Many of the institutions visited regarded the ability to communicate in writing as a fundamental tool, absolutely necessary for any college student. This point is difficult to argue. Like any statement of absolutes, however, it seems a bit extreme. Persons who hold this position may tend to (1) overcredit the ability to be a creative writer when the content of the narrative is just as important as how it is presented, (2) negate the crediting of products, per se, such as paintings, photographs, or pieces of music, and (3) make it difficult to credit a competence such as interviewing which is more accurately demonstrated than explained in writing.

As an example of "the creative writer versus the content of the writing" there follows a series of excerpts from one student's narrative of what she derived from a trip to Europe:

> Always a coterie of five male friends hung around John, sheepishly following, looking like shy remnants of the Kingston Trio or the Lettermen. They were strange—did they think they should be polite to us? Freaks were almost invariably found in co-ed groups, and were not shy, and understood politeness (at least in its ostentatious manifestations) to be without value, hence gauche. The young people we met seemed capable only of stereotypical acting—

either as the machismo-on-the-make 1950's teenager or the
shy, pimply, egghead 1950's teenager. . . .

I realized—America, in 1971, was the capital of the
world. America was Queen in the game of hipness—increasingly the only game in town. We were first, culturally,
and France and England trailed in the awesome wake of
plastic, chrome, chain superstores, non-art, Madison Avenue,
media images. It seemed like a thousand years of mythic
aesthetic and philosophic superiority were petty, shallow,
and irrelevant for Frenchmen—next to America's gleam of
glass skyscrapers and slick magazines—as much as America's
gaudy products and people and ethic were shallow and irrelevant compared to Europe's feudal and religious beauty
for that American tradition of expatriates—T. S. Eliot, Ezra
Pound, Hemingway, and the rest of the line. . . .

He fell in love with me, I think, because he felt I
was a child beyond that door; and maybe I held it open for
him. I was full of life, and he thought he was full of death.
I had felt together with all those eager, tired people at the
Centre de Tourism (people who might stumble into a
Fellini adventure that night when all they wanted was a
soft bed) and I had thrown back my head and laughed.
When he saw me there laughing, he said later, he thought
"You are in color, and all the rest are in black and white."

Of course he was not full of death; he was just full
of beautiful words and ideas that sometimes had no anchor.
I was an anchor. The metaphors don't mix—maybe one
metaphor can't hold the complexity of it: I was a door into
a child-world of ignorant sensualness; and I was an anchor
to secure his floating abstractions down to the palpable
earth. . . .

We left our respective groups, got on his cycle and
road down the coast, then cut through the hills, taking all
the time in the world. Shaking cold, tired on the bike coming into Grasse, little town with a big perfume factory filling
the air. Cycle on cobblestones, little hotel, lots of stairs,
sometimes an ancient lift. Double beds, Jay's pipe and
cherry tobacco on the old walnut table next to my passport
and wallet. Restaurant, French bread, wine, fish, camembert cheese; a French lady feeding her tiny poodle, holding
it in her lap at the restaurant. Cycle flying around the curbs,

hills, villages with red roofs, Jay, enthralled, big bathtubs, brown rough toilet paper. Petite déjeuner—croissants and milky coffee, crumbs in the bed and Jay in the bed in the morning. Charcuteries, boulangeries, "Bonjour, madame," when we entered a store, "Bonjour, madame," when we left. We saw movies—commercials at the beginning, and awful travelogues. The laundromat, with French movie magazines, the children playing in the laundry baskets and shyly talking to us. The cycle, four hours in the shaking sun; we stop, still vibrating, have a single beer on empty stomachs and the world softens, yet lifts; everything blurred but each sensation magnified—sound of glasses clinking, smell of the bike we've carried in on our bodies, my back against the chair. . . .

The faculty advisor wrote the following in support of awarding credit: "I would like to endorse S's petition for Life Experience Seminar (LES) credit. I know her work quite well and can attest to her seriousness as a writer and a student of a certain kind of cultural history. She has managed, I think, genuinely to integrate her education around themes of human identity and cultural change. The other-cultural experience she describes forms a significant part of this education, and the level of insight she has reached is in many ways quite remarkable, certainly well beyond the average of those who have traveled under LES auspices. The paper she has written formally demonstrates systematic thought sufficient to warrant academic credit."

When one reads the entire piece of writing, reproduced as Narrative II at the end of this chapter, one becomes quite aware that the author is a sensitive, insightful young woman, who might receive credit in a number of academic disciplines for this experience and for her ability to identify learnings. The whole narrative is presented so that readers from a number of disciplines can form their own opinions about whether her writing merits credit.

S's greatest ability, however, is that she can write. It is difficult to imagine how her insights and sensitivities would be communicated if her creative writing talent were less than what it is. This question, of course, does not pose a problem for her but would for another person with equally keen insights who did not have the same command of the language.

There is nothing particularly startling or new about this problem. Bright, sensitive, insightful students who also can express themselves creatively have always been a joy. The person who has the insights and sensitivities yet cannot present them in quite as creative a way has the opportunity in a class over a period of time to demonstrate the learning. But this person is at an obvious disadvantage when there is only one event or statement which will demonstrate the learning.

It is quite possible in a prior learning workshop to assist the student who has difficulty with written expression. This can also be handled in individualized tutorials. However, regardless of the amount of assistance, some people will never express themselves as creatively as others. It is doubly important to bear this in mind when the written narrative is the only or primary vehicle of documentation. A constant distinction needs to be made between what has actually been learned and how well it is communicated. I am not trying to establish an either-or dichotomy, only to stress content. If the student is requesting credit for creative writing, then of course the ability to write is emphasized more than it would be if the student wanted credit for another specific content area.

The second problem created by an overemphasis on the written narrative is the negative effect it has on product assessment. For certain programs, the product itself has no intrinsic value. The only creditable value is the student's ability to communicate what has been learned in writing. Such a position is extremely difficult to justify. The limits it places on defining who is an educated person seem absurd, for it implies that only people who can explain what they do in writing are to be considered educated. Although the ability to express oneself in writing is important, it is against all reason to assume that only those who can explain what they have learned from what they do are educated. Most painters, sculptors, composers, performers, as a matter of fact, could write about learning achieved through the performance of their art. The point is that their art has intrinsic value apart from those explanations which should be able to be assessed.

Overemphasizing the written narrative also poses a third and somewhat fuzzier problem. There are a multitude of professional competences which seem to be better assessed and validated by demonstration than by written explanations. Interviewing skill is a good example. The written narrative can get the student to think about and explain the theoretical aspects of interviewing. Concepts such as rapport, eye-contact, selective listening, feedback, nonverbal communication could be described and discussed in their proper order. The student might even be able to construct a model interview. But writing about interviewing, no matter how sophisticated, is quite different from conducting a successful interview. Most programs which credit such learning depend on third-party evaluation to corroborate this kind of skill. At best, this evaluation is an accurate description of how the third-party expert views the student's performance. At worst, it is vague generalities which state that the student has empathy, can establish rapport, and "is a great interviewer."

Although third-party corroboration is helpful, it should not take the place of direct observation. Some competences may not be able to be demonstrated without great cost or upheaval. Most, however, like interviewing, can be demonstrated quite easily by role playing or simulations of other kinds. If third-party corroboration is the only method available, it should be carried out by a panel of experts, each of whom uses the same rating scale. This procedure minimizes the vague and noncommittal kinds of responses so often received.

One of the most fascinating uses of the student narrative is to document and credit learning which results in self-growth or maturation. The few programs involved in this area are attempting to legitimate with adults something which higher education has always said it did for adolescents. One of the major reasons higher education is caught in a four-year baccalaureate time frame is maturation. Adolescents are supposed to grow to young adulthood through the four years of college. In addition to amassing a body of knowledge, young people are to be ready to don their adult roles with their graduation robes. While this objective has been a stated or tacit assumption, the maturation process supposedly taking place during the four college years has seldom been evaluated; it is merely assumed.

Thus, the New Resources Program at the College of New Rochelle is reflecting an old tradition when it states that the creditable aspect of experience is that portion which the student can analyze and reflect upon. Furthermore, such reflection must demonstrate that *the student has learned something about himself and his world.* The written narratives at New Rochelle are called the autobiographies and most are quite lengthy. They also are sometimes painful and often joyful. One student wrote in her foreword, "From the outset, I felt overwhelmed by the task of reflecting in an analytical way on the thirty-two-year span of my life. . . . Through the process of preparing this portfolio, my belief has been confirmed that one encounters certain events and choices in life which are, in fact, decisive factors in one's life. These events may be friendly or hostile, but one's response to them has the power to shape the future."

There is an ongoing struggle within the minds of these budding autobiographers. What shall I include? What shall I leave out? What is too private to share? How can I make public that which is private? The directors of programs which encourage the autobiography report that students can learn to distinguish between the private and the public. One director explained it in this way, "We're not interested in the very private. We suggest to the student that 'you sense yourself in a public realm. What is your participation in society? How have you controlled social forces and how have you lost to them?' Many people wrestle with the question of authority and the behavior of institutions. So, on the one hand we are trying to be autobiographical, while, on the other, acutely socially analytical." Nevertheless a good deal of private material does come out and many students see this emergence as helpful, as cathartic, and as nonthreatening. Their struggles usually end in feelings of satisfaction.

It is due to the vast changes in societal norms in the past

twenty years that such self-disclosure is now possible. Whereas psychotherapy was once an extremely private mechanism to cure the mentally ill, many of today's varied forms of therapy presume one starts from a healthy base and gets healthier. The growth groups, encounter and sensitivity groups allow people to focus openly on what they have learned about themselves. This is true for self-growth as well as growth with and in relation to others in a public rather than private realm (London, 1974). It is possible, therefore, to talk of personal growth not only in relation to intellectual activities but also in terms of emotional awareness. The *content* of this learning becomes emotional awareness of self in relation to self and others as expressed as a *learned set of insights and behaviors.*

Certain of the helping professions have used this level of learned insight as part of their curricula for many years. For example, one of the essential elements of application to graduate schools of social work is an autobiographical essay which specifically looks for learned insights. Once admitted, the graduate social work student is continuously evaluated in this area through all of the field work and many of the classroom activities. Though crediting this kind of prior learning is steadily increasing, the criteria against which these learned insights are measured are a bit slow in coming. For this reason, some caution needs to be exercised in moving ahead. The narrative can and does provide excellent raw data for evaluating learned insights. The criteria used to assess them are not always clarified ahead of time, but the student is entitled to know the parameters.

At present, most instructions for the autobiographical essay are not very specific. Is this because faculty do not wish to limit the student's reflective behavior by establishing too narrow guidelines or because criteria have not been thoroughly thought through? The answer is probably somewhere between. Fordham University's EXCEL Program uses the following instructions for Part 2 of a three-part outline. Students are to prepare: "An *autobiographical essay,* beginning at whatever point in life the student deems appropriate, which includes under individual subheadings full descriptions and analyses of the areas in which the student believes life experience credit is deserved. There is no prescribed length for these descriptions. The important thing is that they communicate fully and effectively your analysis of what you have learned." Fordham has produced some of the finest portfolios for the assessment of prior learning to be found anywhere. Much staff time goes into helping students prepare not only the autobiographical essay, but the entire portfolio. The writing reproduced as Narrative I at the end of this chapter is an excellent example of a focused essay (in this instance focused on police work) which describes learning.

Continuing Education Unit (CEU)

After years of abortive attempts, the continuing education and noncredit field has established a unit of measure known as the Continuing Education Unit (CEU). Finally, someone who has taken numerous worthy noncredit courses can receive some recognition for this effort for purposes of employment or various other goals. The National Task Force which established the CEU used contact hours as the basis for crediting, in much the same way as the Carnegie credit unit does. But here, some educators argue, the similarity ends. They assert that the CEU is meant to be entirely distinct and apart from the credit unit, that it was never meant to be equated with credit and never will be. Another group believes this position is too rigid; if the receiving institution wishes to translate CEUs into credit units, it has every right to do so.

Obviously, this argument is going to have far-reaching effects on the crediting of prior learning in the years to come. Institutions need to keep a number of things in mind as they begin to deal with the CEU. The CEU measures attendance and exposure. So does the credit hour, especially as more and more institutions move into pass/fail or credit/no credit grading systems. The CEU does not claim to be a measure of learning. The credit hour does, but short reflection will raise some questions about this claim. (See earlier discussion on transfer credits.) The only person who is able to relate what has been learned in either situation is the student. If the student is going to be evaluated directly for knowledge, skills, and competences, either unit seems irrelevant. If Carnegie units are going to be accepted without question for credit, then CEUs should be so accepted. To do otherwise would be discriminatory because it sets up the notion that credit units are better than CEUs regardless of how many people say it's not a question of better or worse, but one of "difference." Students who desire a degree will certainly understand which is better if one represents the coin of the realm and the other does not.

It has been argued that most people enrolled in non-credit courses will never be interested in a college degree. This may be true. But what of those who are? They certainly deserve the same consideration as those who enrolled in credit courses. If the argument is that noncredit courses are inferior to credit courses, then let that argument be heard. If they are merely "different," then there should be some equitable means available to reconcile the differences. The problem is new because the CEU is new. The problem is real because students will make it so. The solution is by no means simple but must be found.

Whole Portfolio

Following are two sets of portfolio preparation instructions which are truly exemplary. The first (Exhibit 8) was devised for use at the Long Island Learning Center of Empire State College and the second (Exhibit 9) comes from the University of Wisconsin at Green Bay.

Green Bay's form asks the same questions in a number of areas as are asked regarding employment. Items B through F are repeated for "Volunteer Work," "Hobbies and/or Special Interests," "Travel," "Publications, Reports, Papers, Speeches, Brochures, Pamphlets," and "Other Life Experiences." The academic advisor will give the student as many of these "area" forms as the student thinks appropriate for his/her experiences.

EXHIBIT 8
PORTFOLIO PREPARATION INSTRUCTIONS,
EMPIRE STATE COLLEGE, LONG ISLAND LEARNING CENTER

Introduction

The material that follows is a step by step guide to assist you in preparing the Portfolio upon which your application for advanced standing in the college will be based. The written instructions will be supplemented by live workshops where questions can be answered and students may share problems.

Getting started seems to be the stumbling block, hence the step by step approach. Easy steps first. Harder and more complex steps later. Before you begin I suggest you re-read carefully The Policies and Procedures for Granting Advanced Standing dated June 1, 1973, and the Educational Objectives of the College in the Bulletin on pages 45–55.

Portfolio preparation is an exercise in self-evaluation, organization, and integration. It is an educational experience. It requires you to relate your past learning experiences to your educational goals, to exhibit critical self-analysis, and to demonstrate your ability to present documentation in a clear, concise manner. Remember, the college grants advanced standing for prior LEARNING, not prior experience. As you develop materials, constantly check to make certain you have enunciated or described *learning*. In this respect, your portfolio will differ from a typical resume which describes what you *did* rather than what you *learned*.

How to Gather and Organize Information

CREDITS FROM TRADITIONAL COLLEGES

Validation. You must provide official transcripts to support your request for advanced standing based on credit from traditional colleges. An official transcript is one sent from one college to another. Any transcripts you have in your possession are likely to be "student copies" and not *official*. Please be certain you have asked the registrar of all previous colleges attended to send a transcript to Saratoga.

Evaluation. A one-month full-time Empire State Learning Contract is equal to 3.75 traditional semester credits. In order to translate traditional credits into Empire State months, multiply total number of traditional credits by .267, or for an approximate figure divide by 4. We will convert more accurately for you.

Continued on next page

EXHIBIT 8

Continued from previous page

NONTRADITIONAL OR INFORMAL COURSES

These might include adult education courses, internships, on-the-job training programs, special institutes or conferences.

Validation. Documentation to substantiate your participation in these studies will be required. You should begin immediately to acquire it. This could be in the form of transcripts, letters from the sponsoring organization certifying attendance, a letter from the instructor, etc. Documentation should indicate duration of course, i.e., one two-hour class a week for 15 weeks.

Evaluation. One rule of thumb for estimating credit would be as follows. One credit in a traditional college is earned by attending a one-hour class for 15 weeks and spending two hours of study for each class preparation—a total of 45 hours. A one-month, full-time contract at Empire State is roughly equivalent to a four-credit course.

Life Learning Experience

As you begin work on this section, keep these things in mind: (1) The learnings for which recognition is requested must be defined and clearly expressed. (2) The learnings must be pertinent to your educational goals and consistent with those of the college. (3) Not all learning experiences will be recognized. Think in terms of generally recognized academic competence. Test by asking the question: Why should academic credit be granted? (4) Evidence must be generated to support the learnings described.

(NOTE: *See also "What Kinds of Learning," available from Assessment Secretary.*)

DEVELOPING LEARNING COMPONENTS

Here are a few suggestions to help you begin to think about prior learning and organize the material so it will serve as an outline for your general essay. Your first task is to identify what you know in some organized fashion, i.e., develop learning components. What is a *learning component?* Webster indicates component comes from *componere*—meaning "to put together." The English word is defined as a constituent part or ingredient. In developing learning components for your portfolio, you need to describe the learnings (parts) and put them together. To put it another way: a learning component gives structure to or labels a series of diverse learning activities.

In order to develop learning components it might be helpful to make a list. Don't make it hard work as you begin, but go quickly without being selective. You might begin:

Continued on next page

EXHIBIT 8

Continued from previous page

Law
- (1) General legal procedures, N.Y. State
- (2) Real Estate Law
- (3) Administration, large law firm

Teaching
- (1) Kindergarten through Grade 4
- (2) Audio-visual techniques
- (3) Curriculum development reading

or

Nursing
- (1) Obstetrics:
    - (a) prenatal, postnatal care
    - (b) maternal and child care
    - (c) teaching, counseling

Small Business Development
- (1) General management
- (2) Financial management
- (3) Personnel and employee training
- (4) Customer relations, sales, marketing
- (5) Accounting
- (6) Purchasing
- (7) Production

You might wish to start out in a quite random fashion and need to review your list in order to select and develop learning components. Using the technique above, your general essay will be organized around your learning components.

An alternate approach to developing learning components would be to analyze each experience or job. You would list what you did and what you learned, then review your lists and bring together related learning and develop learning components in this way. If you choose this approach, watch carefully for duplication. Most people proceeding on a career ladder in a specific field inevitably have duplicate experiences from job to job. It is important for you to clearly demonstrate increased learning and scope of responsibility from job to job.

Once you have established your major learning components, you may find it helpful to list each on a separate sheet of paper so you can add other related relevant information to each.

Continued on next page

EXHIBIT 8

Continued from previous page

Validation. Evidence to support your request for advanced standing will be needed for each learning component. On each of your sheets you will need to explain where and how the learning took place and the documentation to support your request. The evidence might include written examinations, licenses, works of art, performance observed and evaluated by an expert, observation reports from employers or supervisors. These are more fully described in "Policies and Procedures for Granting Advanced Standing Based on Prior Learning" dated June 1, 1973, which is in your Orientation packet or in the Bulletin of the college.

A special word is in order about observation reports from employers, supervisors, or co-workers. These will not be the usual letters of recommendation. They will need to substantiate the learnings involved. To assist you in requesting these letters, the college has a form letter it will send on your behalf.

When you are ready for the College to make these requests, please write out names and addresses, include your own name on the sheet, and send or give it to the Assessment Secretary. Women should remember to include their maiden name if their records would be listed under that name. When the letters are received they will be held for you at the Center. The original will be included in your portfolio.

Your work sheets will now look something like this:

Human Relations	Place Learned	Documentation
Organizing groups	Dir. of Volunteers,	Letter:
around task to be	Nassau Hospital	Mr. J. Jones
done	1963–64	Administrative
		Director

Evaluation. Each experience must now be translated into a request for a specific amount of advanced standing—one month, three months, and so on, followed by a rationale as to the logic behind the request. Judgments about advanced standing for prior learning will have as their frame of reference generally accepted expectations of standards for college-level work.

Most students will feel uncertain about evaluating the amount of advanced standing to be assigned to a particular learning component. Some possible guidelines follow. You are encouraged to use them. Assistance in this area will be provided by the college through the faculty and staff as well as outside experts.

(1) Internship equivalence: The experience might be viewed as

Continued on next page

EXHIBIT 8

Continued from previous page

equivalent to a formal internship. For example, teaching experience could be given credit as being a substitute for student-teaching in traditional programs.

(2) Contract content equivalence: The logic might be that the learning experiences represent the equivalent of what would be required in an Empire State Contract of a given length.

(3) Course content equivalence: The learning experiences might be the equivalent of a specified number of traditional courses. The credit equivalence should be more than the months requested to allow for over-estimation. For example, if you say what was learned would equal four to six traditional courses, it would be advisable to request 2–4 months.

On each of your experience sheets you should indicate:

Credit Requested .... and Rationale or Criterion ....

You now have all the raw material necessary to develop your general essay.

GENERAL ESSAY

There are as many ways of writing the essay as there are students and, indeed, it should reflect one's individuality. Whatever your style, a basic outline will be helpful.

An opening statement describing your long-range plans and specific educational objectives in the college, followed by a brief statement indicating the total amount of advanced standing requested. In essay form you then describe the past learning experiences for which you are requesting credit, indicating how these are related to your educational plans or career goals and to each other. The order of the description should be: college credit, life learning experience including the informal courses as they are related.

As you complete the description of each segment for which you are requesting credit, include your rationale and the specific number of months requested. You should also note the documentary material substantiating that learning component. Example: 3 months requested (Appendix A No. 7–8).

Appendix. Your general essay will be followed by an appendix containing your documents of evidence. A table of contents for your appendix documents, listing them in the order noted, would follow the general essay. College transcripts should precede other documents. For example:

Continued on next page

EXHIBIT 8

Continued from previous page

Appendix A—Transcript, Nassau Community College
Appendix B—Letter, Mr. John Jones, Dir.,
     Nassau County Hospital

PROGRAM OF STUDY

The program of study, which sets forth your educational goals, the learning and competencies you have already achieved that are applicable to your goals, and those learning activities still to be undertaken in the college, is the key to your application for advanced standing and the evaluation of your portfolio. The program of study will describe a "major," an area of concentration, organizing theme or special emphasis which will be pursued to levels of substantial depth and complexity. (For further information see Policies and Procedures for Program of Study, dated June 1, 1973.) It will be developed in consultation with your mentor. Your program of study will be included in your portfolio and approved by the Evaluation Committee. Please be certain to include a time frame in your program of study. A sample form for the program of study is found below.

TRANSCRIPT STATEMENT

When your general essay is completed, your evidence in order, your program of study approved by your mentor, you will prepare your transcript statement.

This will be part of your permanent record in the college and will be forwarded to graduate schools if you should apply for admission. You will want to prepare this document carefully and neatly, making certain it reflects your competence and learning. A completed transcript will be found below.

The transcript statement also contains a summary of the learning activities section of your program of study. Please be certain to indicate a time frame for each of these learning activities, i.e., three months full-time or four months half-time.

Getting It All Together

Most students work on their portfolios over a considerable period of time. They become intimately acquainted with each page and document and understand their interrelationships. Members of the assessment committee do not have this advantage, hence it is most important that your portfolio is carefully organized so the stranger can follow it logically and identify substantiating evidence easily.

Continued on next page

EXHIBIT 8

Continued from previous page

Page one will be a table of contents that will look like this:

TABLE OF CONTENTS

1. Transcript Statement .... page ....
2. Program of Study .... page ....
3. General Essay .... page ....
4. Appendix Contents .... page ....

Put your documents in order that far. Then gather your supporting evidence and arrange it in the following order. Traditional college transcripts, then supporting evidence for the learning components from life experience in the order in which they are described in the essay. You can now number the pages beginning at the table of contents consecutively. Then make up a table of contents for the Appendix describing each document and indicating its page.

Note: Sample portfolios, learning components, programs of study, transcript statements, supporting letters or letters of recommendation, are available for *reference* from the Assessment Secretary.

EXHIBIT 8a

APPLICATION FOR APPROVAL FOR PROGRAM OF STUDY

Student's Name: .... Soc. Sec. #: ....

Please give a description of: (a) the student's *Past Educational and/ or Occupational Experience* and activities undertaken while enrolled at Empire State College, or prior to enrollment, or both; (b) the *Major Purposes, Interests, Plans* or aspirations the student wants to pursue; and (c) the *Major Areas and Activities To Be Undertaken,* the mentors with whom the student will work, the organized programs, field experiences, or

Continued on next page

EXHIBIT 8a

Continued from previous page

other major resources to be used, and the general time requirements projected. Do not spell out in detail the particular learning contracts to be undertaken, but provide a clear framework within which the pertinence of these particulars will be apparent. Organize the application statement under the three headings italicized above. Use traditional pages as necessary.

The application for program approval will accompany your portfolio. The program will be worked out with your mentor's assistance.

Note: When writing Program of Study following the instructions above, under (a) summarize *briefly* and narratively your past educational/occupational experience. You need not go into the kind of detail required in your general essay. Also be certain to include the number of months full-time or part-time for each learning activity or contract to be undertaken in the college.

Learning Center Signatures:

Student: ....

Committee Chairman: ....

Assoc. Dean: ....

Date Approved: ....

EXHIBIT 8b

TRANSCRIPT STATEMENT FOR ADVANCED STANDING

Student .... SS # .... Date ....

Summary of Credits:

Nassau Community College	45 cr.	(liberal Arts)
Queens College	9 cr.	(Social Sciences)
	54 cr.	

Months Requested: 14

Continued on next page

EXHIBIT 8b

Continued from previous page

Work and Life Experience (major areas of competence, learning components each, and references to documentation):

    Law   1962–66......

        General civil procedure, wills, probate court proceedings (Doc. #7–8)

        Administration large law firm, Labor law (Doc. #4–5)

        Real Estate law (Doc. #10)

        Research for article *Is the Death Penalty Constitutional?* (Doc. #11)

               Months Requested: 3

    Business   1966–72

        Organization and management (Doc. #1–6)

        Personnel and employee training

        Sales, customer relations, marketing

        Accounting

        Production

               Months Requested: 4

Total Advanced Standing Requested: 21 months

Program of Study Summary:

    My goal is to prepare myself to enter law school. Work at Empire State will include an historical study of American Political Thought from Colonial times to the present (3 months full-time), studies in party politics and the legislative process (3 months full-time), constitutional law and civil liberties (2 months full-time). I also plan studies in sociology and criminology (3 months full-time). My mentor is John Jones.

Decision of Assessment Committee:

    Committee Signatures ....

    Associate Dean .... Date ....

EXHIBIT 9

GUIDELINES FOR PORTFOLIO PREPARATION
UNIVERSITY OF WISCONSIN AT GREEN BAY

AT GREEN BAY

Documentation

Documents normally used to verify learning experiences:

Education and/or Training

Transcripts, diplomas, certificates of completion, program descriptions, course descriptions

Military Experiences

DD-214—certificates of completion for service schools and USAFI courses

Work Experiences

Job descriptions, letters from employers verifying dates of employment, certificates of completion or letters from employers certifying completion of in-service training programs, workshops, seminars, licenses or certificates held

Volunteer Work

Letters from officers, directors, ministers, priests, school officials verifying participation and the duration of the participation

Hobbies and/or Special Interests

Certificates of excellence, awards received, letters from other participants

Travel

Photos, slides, films

Publications, Reports, Papers

A copy

Examples

The following is an example of experiences used and the documents presented to verify the experiences of a registered nurse:

(1) Graduation from a school of nursing (verified by her transcript and diploma).

(2) Extensive in-service training (verified by certificates of completion and letters from directors of in-service training).

(3) Work experience as a nurse in Wisconsin, California, and Colorado (verified by job descriptions and letters from Personnel Director).

Continued on next page

EXHIBIT 9

Continued from previous page

(4) Completion of seminars and workshops (verified by certificates of completion).

(5) European travel (verified by discussion with her, slides, and photographs).

The following is an example of experiences used and the documents presented to verify the experiences of a businessman:

(1) Graduation from a technical school (verified by his transcript).

(2) Credits earned at a four-year college (verified by his transcript).

(3) Workshops, institutes and seminars completed (verified by diplomas and certificates of completion).

(4) Work experiences as a junior accountant, internal auditor, company treasurer, company vice-president (verified by job descriptions, letters from Personnel Directors, company financial papers, statements of short-term and long-term company projections and goals).

(5) Community involvement (copies of reports that were written for various committees and groups, copy of testimony given to a congressional subcommittee, letters verifying participation in school board activities).

EXHIBIT 9a

PREPARATION OF THE RESUMÉ

(Use this handout in conjunction with the Credit Based on Experience Form.)

Steps to follow:

(1) Prior to preparing the resumé, look over the current UWGB catalog very carefully and familiarize yourself with the kind of education UWGB is trying to provide and the kinds of learnings and activities that are included in the academic programs. Then think through your background to determine whether you have already, in some formal or informal way, engaged in comparable learnings and activities.

(2) Prepare a resumé of experiences which you think have some aca-

Continued on next page

EXHIBIT 9a

Continued from previous page

demic basis. Include in the resumé formal education and/or training beyond high school; military experiences, if any; work experiences including the in-service training programs, workshops and seminars that have been completed; volunteer work and leadership positions held for school, church, clubs, civic organizations, etc.; hobbies or special interests; travel; and publications, reports or papers prepared for and/or presented to professional organizations, civic organizations, etc.

(3) Bring your resumé to an academic advisor (SS1930—telephone number 2362) who will help you to identify those experiences which seem most appropriate to use in seeking credit.

EXHIBIT 9b

CREDIT BASED ON EXPERIENCE

It is important for you to tell us *what you learned* from your experiences and how this learning relates to courses and/or academic programs at UWGB. However, describe any significant learning experiences, even if you are not sure how they relate to specific courses and/or academic programs. Please use the outline below in preparing and assembling your materials for evaluation.

LEARNING EXPERIENCES

I. Postsecondary Education
   A. Private Vocational-Technical Schools attended:
      (Attach transcripts.)

   B. Public Vocational-Technical Schools attended:
      (Attach transcripts.)

   C. Military Schools attended and USAFI courses completed:

Continued on next page

EXHIBIT 9b

Continued from previous page

(Attach diplomas, certificates of completion, DD-214, course and/or school identifying numbers, dates of attendance and/or completion, military or civilian installation at which education/training occurred.)

D. Two-year and four-year colleges attended:
(Attach transcripts.)

E. Nursing and other professional schools attended:
(Attach transcripts.)

II. EMPLOYMENT
A. List the job(s) you have held or the type(s) of work you have done.

B. How long was each job held or the type of work performed?

C. What percentage of your weekly job or work time was spent in learning? (Consider on-the-job learning, in-service training sessions, workshops, seminars, institutes, etc.)

D. Describe exactly what you learned.

E. To what specific UWGB academic programs and/or courses does each learning experience relate? How does each one relate? (Consider how the learning from your experiences might be equivalent to the content of courses and programs, how your learning might allow you to accelerate in a subject area—for example, skip introductory courses and immediately enroll in advanced courses—etc.).

F. Explain how what you learned from your work experiences relates to your present educational goals, continues to benefit you, and has contributed to your personal philosophy and outlook.

Narrative I: A New York City Policeman

EDUCATION: Saint Patrick Academy
                    Saint Francis Preparatory
                    City College of New York
                    Rockland Community College
                    New York University
                    Fordham University

CREDITS: C.C.N.Y., Police Science   6 credits
                    R.C.C., English I and II   6 credits
                    R.C.C., Elementary Spanish   3 credits
                    N.Y.U., Introduction to Sociology   4 credits

PRESENT STATUS: Credits earned at Fordham University   36 credits
                 Transfer credits   19 credits
                 Total credits earned   55 credits

EMPLOYMENT EXPERIENCE:

Dates	Assignment	Position
July 1957 to June 1960	United States Marine Corps	Infantryman
July 1960 to Jan. 1961	First National City Bank	Teller
May 1961 to Sept. 1961	New York City Police Department, Police Academy	Recruit
Sept. 1961 to Sept. 1966	Tactical Patrol Force	Patrolman
Sept. 1966 to Dec. 1967	Detective Bureau, Safe Loft and Burglary Squads	Detective Investigator

Continued on next page

Narrative I: A New York City Policeman

Continued from previous page

Dec. 1967 to May 1970	Tactical Patrol Force	Sergeant Supervise Patrol
April 1970 to Oct. 1971	Delehanty Institute	Lecturer
May 1970 to May 1971	Detective Bureau, Narcotics Division 6th District	Sergeant Supervise Detectives
May 1971 to Sept. 1971	Detective Bureau, Narcotics Division 3rd District	Lieutenant Commanding Officer
Sept. 1971 to Sept. 1972	Intelligence Division Organized Crime Section, Narcotic Intelligence Unit	Lieutenant Commanding Officer
Sept. 1972 to April 1973	Intelligence Division Administrative Section	Lieutenant Commanding Officer
April 1973 to Present	Intelligence Division Major Probe Unit	Lieutenant Commanding Officer

Writing this paper attesting to my worth on the academic market, in the coinage of college credits, is a particularly difficult chore. I am torn between the need to write and the many reasons to refrain.

There exists a dichotomy of motivation:

a. It is alien to my nature to "blow my own horn." (This is probably due to the overemphasis, in early schooling, on the distorted view of the Christian ethic of humility, which was translated into self-effacement.)

b. It is a surrender to a credentially oriented society, and as a practicing policeman I have seen too many of my colleagues pursue academic laurels at the expense of providing good police service. I hold such a practice to be immoral.

c. It is distasteful to me to seek or importune special favor or recognition.

d. I consider serious self-evaluation the only valid measure of a man.

Continued on next page

Narrative I: A New York City Policeman

Continued from previous page

e. I feel some remote kinship to the character in Plato's "Allegory of the Cave"—"And if they were in the habit of conferring honours among themselves on those who were quickest to observe the passing shadows . . . do you think he would care for such honours. . . ?"

f. I have been fortunate enough to have achieved a certain level of self-actualization; to descend the ladder of the hierarchy of needs in pursuit of recognition seems inappropriate.

Nevertheless, I believe in the ability of the committee to reach an honest appraisal on the matter and so I submit this paper. (Even this sounds a bit Kafka.)

The reasons to rejoice in the preparation of this document include that:

a. As a pragmatist I need the credits.

b. As an existentialist my experience is, in fact, me.

c. It is a good vehicle for forced reflection and self-assessment.

d. As a team player I know there are no "heroes." Hopefully, I shall convey that attitude and avoid self-aggrandizement.

I shall heed then the Talmudic exhortation.

> If I am not for myself, who will be for me?
> If I am for myself only, what am I?
> If not now—when?

I shall try to relate my life experience to the academic disciplines. I make this preamble in mitigation of the ramblings which follow.

Upon graduation from St. Francis Prep. in 1957, I immediately entered the Marine Corps for a three-year enlistment. Depending upon my mood I alternately view this act as a profound blunder of the greatest magnitude or a priceless experience in preparation for life—a finishing school.

Despite the recruiter's claim that "the Marine Corps builds men," I have found that the growing up process has continued to the present. The military experience certainly created a reverence for the value of individuality. Compliance with orders without question poses some serious problems. The effectiveness of such a system in attaining goals is undeniable but the toll on the individual is devastating. Daily headlines point to the need for close scrutiny of such systems, whereas the antithesis of the academic community is startling. Here each student's course is charted by individual

Continued on next page

Narrative I: A New York City Policeman

Continued from previous page

counseling to satisfy the specific and particular needs of one man or woman.

Perhaps my disappointment with the military is a product of my own naiveté, which was illustrated when I chose from a list of possible assignments the Fleet Marine Force—thinking it to be a romantic dress-blue-type detail, traveling the globe guarding admirals and such, sharing vicariously in their pomp through a proximity to power. I was wrong again. It turned out to be the infantry.

The dehumanizing aspects of military activity have become all the more obnoxious in recent days as I realize a growing awareness of the sacredness of the humanity of each man. Even in my present role as a commander of an intelligence squad of the New York City Police Department, I balk at an evaluation process which attempts to place an arbitrary value on a detective's worth. Notwithstanding the need to measure work performance and effectiveness, I see here a challenge to the intrinsic value of every man's real worth, his very humanity, by measuring and grading one facet of his total humanness, the work arena.

Since I have been with the police department since the age of 21, virtually all of my adult life has centered around my work within the department. It may be unfashionable in today's climate to express pride, but I was extremely proud on the day I was sworn. I have since been promoted through the ranks of detective, sergeant, lieutenant, and within days of this writing I will be promoted to the rank of captain. None of these has left fonder memories or greater satisfaction than being selected as a New York City patrolman.

For six years I served as a member of the Tactical Patrol Force, a proud and elite corps of volunteers who perform, almost exclusively, night duty in high-hazard locations. They act as an emergency response team at scenes of public disorder or riot. During these years I served on foot and motor patrol and in plainclothes decoy operations where, on occasion, I donned female attire. Although I thought I looked stunning in "drag," I received no proposals—of marriage that is!

My next assignment was to the Detective Bureau and the highly respected and coveted Safe Loft and Burglary Squad. It was probably in this squad amid the finest detectives in the department that I was bitten by the cops and robbers bug and contracted a chronic case of investigativitis. In a spirit of charity I shall refrain from telling war stories.

I was soon promoted to the rank of sergeant and left the Detective Division to return to the Tactical Patrol Force. While there I supervised

Continued on next page

Narrative I: A New York City Policeman

Continued from previous page

both uniform and plainclothes decoy operations. (By this time the decoys' female attire had been supplanted by the long black coats of Hassidic rabbis with fur-lined hats, theatrical beards, and the like. As the old vaudevillian line goes—I didn't look Jewish so I never suited up.)

In addition to my line or operational duties I was assigned as the training officer for the Tactical Patrol Force, a responsibility which followed me to my next assignment in the Detective Bureau. The duties included the research and preparation of instructional material and lecturing. The topics covered a broad range from the law of arrest, interpretation of the penal law, or code of criminal procedure, to the proper technique for dealing with violent, disorderly, or simply annoying people that the officer might face while on patrol. Since the men concerned were already serving in highly volatile neighborhoods, the exercise of good judgment was essential in avoiding confrontations with explosive potential.

Of course the training function of a police superior is not restricted to the formal structure of a lesson plan or lectures. Rather, it is a daily and hourly responsibility to insure safe and proper performance by the men under one's charge. It is a duty which, if neglected, can cause great personal harm to the man and bring shame and discredit to the department. I take this responsibility of demonstrating proper performance and developing the potential within my associates very seriously.

Before arrests for bribery became the "in" thing for policemen to do, narcotic investigators under my command made more of these arrests than the remainder of the Narcotics Division combined. Included in the list of corruptors finally uncovered were two attorneys. They had, for years, been confounding the criminal justice system by suborning witnesses and bribing policemen. I take great satisfaction in having helped to produce an atmosphere in which the men felt they could take the proper action against corruption without fear of censure from peers or superiors.

The foregoing are primarily concerned with the attitudinal aspects of training. But there is another phase which is even more important to the general public, and that is the development of the skills and knowledge a good policeman or investigator must possess. The citizen expects the policeman to apprehend burglars, recover property, and prevent assaults and robberies.

How does one go about catching a burglar? How does one distinguish stolen property from that legitimately possessed? What does a thief look like? Lombrosso, an early criminologist of the last century, claimed that criminals did have a look about them. He claimed that

Continued on next page

Narrative I: A New York City Policeman

Continued from previous page

physical appearance was an indicator of a criminal bent. He was so totally wrong that today even the police are not likely to call anyone a criminal, until the Supreme Court has pontificated on the final appeal. Unless we can train our novice policeman to accept the fact that criminals, whether committing burglaries, robberies or trafficking in narcotics, are identifiable not because their eyes are too close together but because their *actions* are signposts to a wary observer, no improvement in reducing crime will be forthcoming.

I have seen the criminal "do his thing" while I watched, waited, and arrested. The academician would call it empirical knowledge. Others might call it a sixth sense. But whatever we call it, it must be transmitted to the younger men before they accept complacency with their role. I like to think I have done my share in this regard, by assigning men with complementary skills and personalities together to allow for a trade-off of talent.

I returned to the Detective Division as a sergeant and was assigned to a Harlem narcotics squad. This was not my first assignment to a black community, but it serves to introduce a point.

I have learned about Blackness not from Ellison's *Invisible Man*, nor Cleaver's *Soul on Ice*, nor television documentaries on slum conditions, nor tourist excursions through the black world of 7th Ave. & 125th St.

To me the black experience is real people, the pitiful souls, grown and burly men, products of an educational system which left them incapable of signing their own names to a fingerprint form. The humiliation they felt at this point was greater than that produced by the arrest itself. The total despair and hollowness I have felt at those moments is incommunicable. I have stood face to face with arsonists, militants, and listened while jeering mobs spewed hate and terror on a handful of white and black policemen who represented the cause of all their ills.

I have daily visited the hovels that thousands are forced to call home. I have been to these "homes" to find lost children, to arrest parents selling heroin, to search for weapons or drugs, to stop bleeding or to remove the dead.

I make no claim of being able to empathize with the black American but I can appreciate his economic problem when he returns home from work to find his television and his few meager possessions gone the way of the burglar. His position as "official victim" is unchallenged.

Continuing in a sociological framework, I have marveled at the

Continued on next page

Narrative I: A New York City Policeman

Continued from previous page

cohesiveness of the Hassidic community (an orthodox sect of Judaism with sizeable representation in Bensonhurst, Crown Heights and Williamsburg in Brooklyn and Spring Valley, New York). The ability of this community to effect change and wield influence is out of proportion to its strength of numbers. I have often wondered how so small a group could exercise such seemingly inordinate power. Was historical persecution of the Jews being recompensed by a guilty society? Was it a political block or a political expedient? Was it an economic pressure? Was it a combination of all these things? Or was it simply that they were a group that had a singleness of purpose—a unity which others could well emulate?

Continuing in the behavioral sciences, it would be a fair statement that the daily work of a policeman can be reduced to one word—people. Their humanness transcends age, race, religion, sex, politics, intelligence, sanity and even their criminality.

To find "the person" hidden beneath all the roles he has assumed in life can take a psychiatrist or psychoanalyst years. But as a policeman I have had to find a common ground of communication almost immediately with many types, from the disruptive adolescents that even parents cannot fathom to those less than sane. They are a special problem—such as the lady who was being constantly bombarded from space by secret rays. They take understanding, kindness and time. It's not so difficult to do when you realize—they have no one else.

Even the most militant of demonstrators from the Young Lords to the Neo-Nazi Party become "people" when a dialogue is established to set ground rules at scenes of demonstrations. They almost invariably respond to a request when made in a participative spirit.

I once asked Joseph Columbo, head of an Organized Crime Family, to contain his marchers outside of the Headquarters of the F.B.I. He had tremendous authority over his people. The police had very little. A confrontation seemed inevitable. I explained our requirements to him in a quiet tone and in deference to his real authority over the crowd. Because I rendered what he felt was respect instead of a self-righteous scorn, our demands were met and the demonstrators policed themselves without incident. My relief was not as delicate, however, and he experienced a difficult tour.

The expression of respect for the dignity of an individual has paid dividends even when dealing with hardened criminals who face long jail terms. Very often the proper handling of a prisoner will result in his cooperation with the authorities despite the so-called honor among thieves.

Continued on next page

Narrative I: A New York City Policeman

Continued from previous page

An honest rapport with a felon has provided me with much help. This cooperation is essential in penetrating the closed society in which the successful criminal operates. It tends to verify otherwise unverifiable facts and build stronger cases.

On the other hand, observations of riot and violence leave me with the belief that they must be met with decisive and sufficient force for suppression. To vacillate or issue token response invites disaster, and prolongs and lengthens the damage.

I am fearful that these reminiscences have taken on the pallor of war stories; therefore I shall cease and desist. Suffice to say that I have learned the value of compromise, patience, self-discipline, and above all listening.

On promotion to rank of lieutenant I was retained within the Detective Bureau, an unusual honor for a newly promoted and junior lieutenant, and I was given command of the Midtown Narcotics Squad.

As the commanding officer of this unit I began to direct the efforts of the men away from low-level targets of opportunity to the more difficult long-range investigations of higher echelons of the narcotics distribution system. Our first effort in this direction led to the largest seizure of heroin ever recorded in Queens County.

I am gratified to have been a participant in this and other major investigations, since I feel that a good investigator is rare enough to be placed on the endangered species list.

Shortly thereafter I was transferred to the Intelligence Division and given the job of organizing a Narcotic Intelligence Unit within the Organized Crime Section. I left the operational end of things, or so I thought, to put together a comprehensive picture of narcotics conditions throughout the city and at all levels of the distribution system.

It was in this assignment that I found the greatest satisfaction. The team assembled to do this job played a critical and major role in immobilizing the largest network of drug distributors in the United States.

My instructions, on arriving in September of 1971, were to establish a narcotics intelligence capability within the division. The personnel assigned to the effort included three sergeants and eighteen investigators. Only four members of the unit had previous narcotics experience. To say we started from scratch would understate it. In fact, we had to overcome preconceived notions and erroneously drawn conclusions regarding the drug distribution systems extant in the metropolitan area.

Years of inadequate attention to the narcotics problem had created

Continued on next page

Narrative I: A New York City Policeman

Continued from previous page

a vacuum of information on the subject. Pseudo-experts had for years been touting a false brand of information, partially prompted by greed and involvement with the very criminals they were charged with immobilizing.

To distill fact from fancy and present an accurate and honest appraisal of our posture as it regards narcotics is still a difficult job. The department became entrenched in the myths created by these inept or corrupt narcotics officers. Many ranking officers still fail to see the problem and to the extent to which they remain ignorant of their problem they shall fail to develop solutions.

In each major probe conducted by our unit we worked in a task force concept with the federal, state and local law enforcement agencies. This was a complete break with tradition in which each agency jealously guarded its own cases. We provided the leadership in bringing District Attorneys from each borough, adjoining counties and states, and included the United States attorney's office and federal drug agencies in a combined effort against a common enemy.

We did not do this alone but we were the focal point, the neutral non-arrest unit, that threatened no one's position. Acting as a catalyst, we prompted other agencies and units to let down their defenses and cooperate. In retrospect and by comparison I can appreciate the problem of the United Nations in reaching the most mundane resolutions. I am happy to report that this cooperation is now the order of the day thanks to the successes we realized.

One major contribution in which I take great pride was the exploitation and development of television as an investigative tool. Our efforts were those of the novice but we were sincere. The product may lack the polish of a network production but in the final analysis this may redound to its credit.

Our stated goal in using television was to "deliver a message" in an unusual and dramatic way. If the message was received the necessary action would follow. It worked time and again. Submitted with this paper is a montage of other video tapes which were addressed to: street-level narcotic sales, high-level narcotic distributions training sessions, and intelligence referral information.

In October of 1972 the Intelligence Division was reorganized and I was assigned as the commanding officer of the Administration Section. The duties were basically to act as an executive officer to the Chief of Intelligence. They included all phases of managerial responsibility ranging

Continued on next page

Narrative I: A New York City Policeman

Continued from previous page

from planning, budgeting, report review, monitoring of federal grants, and developing personnel recruitment and training programs for the division.

The umbrella of this command also covered the technical services unit which is responsible for the installation of wire taps and bugs for the entire department. A video and photographic capability was also included in this responsibility. The need for close attention to such activities to prevent misuse and maintain security of installations is highlighted by the present "Watergate Hearings."

Although half of my experience in the department has been in the capacity of a superior officer, the post of Commanding Officer, Administration Section, was a new experience since it was almost totally staff in nature as opposed to the line functions with which I was familiar. I recognize the need for both functions but if I had my druthers I'd rather manage a line operation.

In May of this year I was assigned to develop a Major Probe Unit for the Intelligence Division. It was intended to act as an intelligence system in microcosm concerned with a limited subject—Hispanic Organized Crime—to demonstrate the feasibility of a modular approach to the overall responsibilities of the Intelligence Division. If successful, modules comprised of collectors, analysts, and investigators would attend to each specific area of concern to the department, e.g., organized crime families, black liberation army, hijack rings, labor racketeering, etc. Plans are presently being drawn up to expand this concept based on the success of this pilot.

Although most of my work experience has been within the department, in April of 1970 I became associated with a private training institute as an instructor-lecturer in their Police Promotion Course. The course of instruction included principles of management, supervision, penal law, criminal procedure law, criminal investigation, reading and graph interpretation, and topical developments in the criminal justice field. The hoped for results were students capable of passing civil service tests for sergeant, lieutenant, and captain.

I continued in this capacity for eighteen months, during which time I became aware of the fact that the teacher learns more than the student. This experience was a contributing factor in returning to school. From behind the lectern, addressing from 25 to 100 students, I felt somehow inadequate, as though I lacked some sort of qualification or credential. Obviously I would not have been there had I not demonstrated some

Continued on next page

Narrative I: A New York City Policeman

Continued from previous page

ability, but there existed a void, I thought; perhaps a baccalaureate would fill the vacuum.

While I felt a certain sense of inadequacy I also felt in total control of my subject. My confidence bordered on conceit. I knew what a candidate for promotion in the police department must do to succeed. Sacrifice and work and then work harder.

For almost two years I had studied four hours each day, seven days each week, mostly between the hours of 2 a.m. and 8 a.m. (no noise or traffic, you see). If this seems a bit exaggerated a talk with a few fellow sufferers will erase any doubt. Apparently, a boss is something I had to be.

The work paid off when the results of the sergeant's examination placed me within the 10 highest marks from a field of 18,000 competitors. This foundation enabled me to pass the lieutenant's examination as third highest man from a field of 3,000 competitors.

The examination for captain produced less spectacular results but I passed. So who's complaining? Considering the fact that I have served approximately 12 years with the department and the rise from patrolman to captain will have taken less than 6 years, I feel satisfied that my hard work has been rewarded.

It is fashionable in some circles to scorn the Civil Service system, especially in the areas of testing and promotion. I do not wish to champion this system but I must comment on what I see as one overriding advantage. It does not produce a cadre of geniuses or superior intellects, but neither does college. It does not produce true leaders, but neither does a West Point or Annapolis. It does, however, produce a select number of determined and self-disciplined aspirants for promotion, who are willing to work according to the rules of the game. This self-discipline is so critically needed that whatever other failings Civil Service may have they are overshadowed.

During my association with the private training institute I was instrumental in developing an Audio Cassette Course of instruction, a sample of which accompanies this report.

Through my insistance the program got under way and drew in considerable revenue. Here is where I learned a lesson in economics, business administration, and white-collar chicanery. The institute has failed to comply with a contract entered into with me and litigation is presently under way. Consequently you will find no validation of my performance with the institute in these pages. Despite the distasteful business of being cheated I thoroughly enjoyed developing and recording the tapes.

Continued on next page

Continued from previous page

I recently completed a course, given exclusively by cassette, at New York University. I had hoped to learn something of the techniques employed but I was disappointed to receive nothing more than recorded lectures. I feel that the medium of cassette education deserves its own format and I agree with Boswell when he quotes Johnson, *"I cannot see that lectures can do so much good as reading books from which the lectures are taken."*

I have found New York City Cops to be the toughest audience imaginable. The baptism of fire I experienced in lecturing before them has given me a confidence in public speaking which has supported me in addressing angry Harlem community groups demanding better police service as well as in attending conferences with agency heads of the federal, state, and local criminal justice system.

In fact, I recently addressed a conference hosted by Major Lindsay at Gracie Mansion, briefing the editorial staff members of the news media on narcotic conditions. After a time I began to feel as though I belonged there.

As any reader of this document can attest I have a high opinion of myself and of my accomplishments. My wife calls it conceit. Fortunately I am realistic enough to accept the fact that no one man can do much on his own. I have been fortunate in my career to have been associated with patrolmen, detectives, superiors, and civilians who have been generous enough to take the time to help me, humor me, or simply tolerate me. For this I am thankful and indebted.

It would be unforgivable to spin so lengthy a tale of life experience without once recognizing the only really important elements of any man's life, his family. Mine is composed of a wife-typist, an 18-month-old son, and an anticipated arrival circa January 1974.

Narrative II: A European Trip

My formal preparation for my European trip included a semester of college French and a course called "Human Identity: Hesse and Ionesco."

Continued on next page

Narrative II: A European Trip

Continued from previous page

In addition, the semester prior to my leaving I spent intensive hours in studying aspects of French and European life in order to allow me to choose which program I wanted to be in (since I had virtually the whole world to choose from) and to prepare me for the cultural shock of adjustment. This semester's work included a couple of formal evenings with returned foreign students and many hours of informal discussion with students who had been abroad. In addition, I spent several hours a week talking to my Antioch Abroad advisor or studying in the Abroad library to select and learn about a foreign country. The reading I did included general works but mainly centered on term papers, job descriptions, and reports from students who had been to France and other countries. These readings related directly to me because they were about what other students had learned about the European and French cultures as well as their personal feelings of culture shock and adaptation to their time abroad. Not only was this fascinating, it was necessary since, aside from our flight arrangements, all arrangements for travel, accommodations, meals, financing in Europe, and so on were the responsibility of the student. The Antioch advisors arranged the matriculation in specific foreign schools for students and had permanent advisors in major foreign cities who could be contacted in emergencies, but the day-to-day getting about in a foreign country was entirely up to the student.

"You will gain some understanding of the similarity and diversity in the world. . . . The importance of the other region program is in the experience it provides you . . . not only concerned with observations on the day-to-day life of the area you visit but . . . centered on a previously determined topic of comparison."

Before going to Europe I had had one year of high school and one semester of French at Antioch College. My original intention was to go to an intensive language school in Besancon (in Northwest France) for three months, and then to go to London where I would be in an Antioch Abroad program in Creative Writing.

My whole career, including the European trip, has had an inevitable focus: human personality and interrelationships, including the value structures and cultural assumptions of particular individuals. It is my nature automatically to bring all learning to this personal level. The social sciences have an inadequate structure for understanding human personality or for clarifying personal value structures. Thus I am equally interested in both the social sciences and in the humanities areas of literature, philosophy, art, history, etc., as the key areas for understanding modern man and myself

Continued on next page

Continued from previous page

and my relation to my fellow modern person. Appropriately, I am an Analysis Synthesis concentrator. My "previously determined topic of comparison," obviously, was human identity and value systems.

I was, before going to Europe, deeply immersed in the "counterculture" at Antioch College (the "hippest college east of San Francisco"). Thus in Europe the counterculture forces, which I shall refer to as the freak culture, for want of a better name, were clearly present along with the bedding of WASP culture of my family. For example, I not only hungered for the sight of a MacDonald's hamburger to cure my culture shock or homesickness, I was at least as ravenous for someone who could quote Fritz Perls for me, or show me where I could get granola. I did not so much desire these manifestations of my culture, as a person whom I could relate to with these commonalities understood.

I deplaned in Luxembourg with Sara, my Antioch roommate of a short duration, who knew French relatively well. We had three weeks to waste before our language program began in Besancon. We attacked the usual problems of restauranteese (do we leave a tip? do you know anything about wine? how to summon a waiter? etc.), of finding a room, understanding train schedules, exchanging money, and so on. We went to Paris, went to the Louvre, took a boat trip down the Seine, and did a few other touristy things. That was virtually the end of my sightseeing—in the traditional sense—in Europe.

Antioch, a college where every other quarter each student leaves campus to get a job in a different environment, breeds a unique culture of its own. I brought from it a peculiar sense of rootlessness, of cut-off relationships and of dunking experiences. On the basis of that experience it did not take more than two weeks in Europe to make me irritated and depressed with hotels and sightseeing, with shallow confrontations of tourist-attuned Parisian proprietors of shops, hotels, and restaurants.

I began to dislike Sara—I thought of myself as more experienced, "liberated," and mature than she was and violently disliked the reliance I was forced to place on her with her superior French. I had the constant distinct feeling that she did not correctly follow directions for instance, but I could only do far worse than she at interpreting the rapid French we were bombarded with. I was no doubt a horrendous person to be with then. In this emotional climate we agreed to seek contact with students or someone who might be somewhat analagous to us freaks.

We located the student section of Paris and asked directions of a group of young people sitting in a cafe. There were about 10 men and one woman, smoking Gauloises and looking like they were posing for a

Continued on next page

Narrative II: A European Trip

Continued from previous page

magazine ad for American cigarettes. I had to come to France to find the models for that ad. This epitomizes the gap between my 1971 freaks and French students, that was confirmed in my later contacts: they were stylish. We felt above and beyond that. Women wore bras and dresses, set their hair and used makeup. Men appeared leftovers from the mid-60's Beatles followers, with modest shag haircuts. (To be sure, some such individuals existed, at airports and Lord and Taylor stores, in America; but not in Yellow Springs, Ohio. Antiochians' mothers might have dressed so, with their husbands at Black Panther benefits with Leonard Bernstein and his turtlenecks; but not Antiochians.)

One individual looked different, out of place in the advertisement, or there for comic relief. John wore a flapping Artful Dodger overcoat, jeans, and a tall black top hat. He looked like the Madhatter. It was not the rigorous non-uniform of freaks; more like the costumes of the hippie flower children; but it was a step in the right direction. He talked much more rapidly than anyone else, and even with my French I knew he was using scores of nonsense words. More than the others he wanted to help us. He set about finding us a place to stay in the student part of town, and kept us under his flapping wing until we left three or four days later. We visited his room, trailed along after his flying figure over half of Paris, and were smuggled into the University cafe under his aegis.

Always a coterie of five male friends hung around John, sheepishly following, looking like shy remnants of the Kingston Trio or the Lettermen. They were strange—did they think they should be polite to us? Freaks were almost invariably found in co-ed groups, and were not shy, and understood politeness (at least in its ostentatious manifestations) to be without value, hence gauche. The young people we met seemed capable only of stereotypical acting—either as the machismo-on-the-make 1950's teenager or the shy, pimply, egghead 1950's teenager.

Felix was different too—he was not really of a separate culture from his elders as we were. When he got into a screaming match with a driver of a car that had nearly run him down one of the countless times he had darted in front of traffic, his voice and demeanor were identical whether the driver was 50 or 20 years old. He seemed not to be afraid, and truly full of hate of *les flics,* as we were afraid and full of hate of policemen. He bawled that they were pigs to their faces, which our real fear would not allow us to. His world was a joke. He did not have the constellation of paranoia, separate perceptions and deviant values that broke off the freaks from the mainstream population.

Continued on next page

Narrative II: A European Trip

Continued from previous page

It was from this group and other individuals that we became acquainted with Frenchmen—

The young kids, they drink beer instead of the good wine of their parents (strange, because freaks smoke pot, do various drugs, but in 1971 they seldom drink—that was the jocks' and the parents' drug—and when they drink they drink wine).

Like John, they often had no fathers; they died in the war.

They went to classes which consisted entirely of lectures, with monstrous crowds of students in each class; they did not know professors nor did they talk in class. (Antiochians had no grades; and the professors either interacted with them with respect for them, or else feared them and failed as teachers.) The French kids feared, even frivolous John dreaded, failing at the University—and failure was an ever-present threat (while we freaks dropped out almost compulsively, to know life as it was outside of academia, to know relevance).

Because—

The most important, necessary goal in their lives was to make money, to succeed in achieving the material, middleclass good life. (We freaks were scathed with that good life's psychic scars; rejected it and at the same time possessed it like nobility possess titles—unquestioningly, as our birthright.) The French, especially the young, wanted to be like Americans—yearned to have our possessions and our glittering insensate acceptance of our richness.

I realized—America, in 1971, was the capital of the world. America was Queen in the game of hipness—increasingly the only game in town. We were first, culturally, and France and England trailed in the awesome wake of plastic, chrome, chain superstores, non-art, Madison Avenue, media images. It seemed like a thousand years of mythic aesthetic and philosophic superiority were petty, shallow and irrelevant for Frenchmen—next to America's gleam of glass skyscrapers and slick magazines—as much as America's gaudy products and people and ethnic were shallow and irrelevant compared to Europe's feudal and religious beauty for that American tradition of expatriates—T. S. Eliot, Ezra Pound, Hemingway, and the rest of the line.

I found many negative opinions of America, from jokes to real resentment. I continually thought I heard the note resounding of a power relationship, where the weak craves, feeds on the strong, and is inevitably oppressed by that sense of weakness, inferiority and need. The weak knows it is his own action that puts him down.

Continued on next page

Narrative II: A European Trip

Continued from previous page

Felix's most treasured possession was a small tape recorder (every freak had some such music machine). But their systems had 24" speakers, not 6" speakers like Felix's. $300 could buy a minimally acceptable system; because drugs and the whole experience had taught us how essential *quality* music was—one could go for a week without sex or dope more easily than without music. Music—good music [artistically and electronically speaking]—was for freaks like color is—necessary, accepted, shedding emotional meaning and definition on the whole environment). I consider that I never heard decent music—meaning decently recorded and amplified music with decent artists and compositions—while in France. How *could* youth exist, and identify with American youth, without this? Felix was so proud of his hipness in having a recorder and a couple of tapes of underground music. His $60 Sony was laughable, had it not been pathetic. His tapes were Hendrix and Cream, but a couple of years old. And compared to the freak's library, with 50 or 100 or 300 albums or tapes. . . . His pride was so great, his friends so envious—I was of course tactful, and admired the bounty he possessed, somewhat appalled by his plight. (An interesting switch that was on the old stereotype of the sophisticated, cultured, subtle European tastefully protecting the naive American from his innocent brazen vulgarity and manifest ignorance and lack of culture.)

Felix had taken LSD—the others were afraid to do that but were tempted. Unlike other commodities it was much more expensive in France than the US: and from Felix's description of a much lower quality. His madness was without seeming purpose other than existential anarchy. Example: he was wedged tightly into a parallel parking place. All 8 (?) of us piled into about 2, and Felix revved the motor and went forward and then backward literally ramming the cars in front and behind until he had banged out enough room to screech out and away. It wasn't a protest of any kind against the other cars—it was done out of gleeful fun.

Sara and I decided to proceed to Besancon, where we had an Antioch/French advisor who would get us a room. We felt in our own apartment there instead of in expensive hotels we would feel less rootless. In Paris and Besancon, whenever we spoke with French youth, they would begin to discuss current issues such as Viet Nam, pollution, and materialism. They invariably recounted how bad the U.S. was in these areas. The conversation always broke down. They pictured the U.S., for instance, as a mass of totally polluted land, because our media so successfully covered the ecology protests—because we the protest culture made these things News.

Continued on next page

Narrative II: A European Trip

Continued from previous page

Similar problems were obvious to me there—the Seine stank as much as the Potomac—the materialism seemed all the more rampant for being unfulfilled. But because their youth were not like us, they could not rightly see the ethos that was mirrored in the Media's coverage of events. I concluded that the actual issues that were at stake during the 60's and early 70's were not so important to our understanding as were our reasons, our mindset that propelled us into protest.

They saw the problems and complaints, but not much of the freedom and liberality that were the background. They would echo some accusations that must have originally come from a Paris *Match* article on the Black Panthers—about the oppression of Blacks—not knowing that the very self-assertion of the Black culture against Black oppression made them so much more beautiful, free and successful than the rather pitiful Algerians and East Indians of France and later England. They were totally out of touch with the subtle currents of freak feeling that the Blacks were a cultural model to be envied, embraced and imitated. After the freaks were so shaped by Black culture, the freak ethic was absorbed into the main culture in many ways (in part causing the "downfall" of freaks as a separate counterculture). They did not realize the position of pride and strength that the Black movement embodied. How could one explain a whole different world, in rotten French? . . . And the conversation especially faltered as the hand under the table reached for the knee. The French hardly even knew of the Feminist movement; saw it at best as a vague joke propagated by a few crazy bra burners.

To jump ahead in the story a bit, it was an incredible relief when I got to England and no longer had males constantly accosting me; there, only foreigners were so obtuse and gauche. Let me cite an example: A Frenchman followed me down a sidewalk in London, saying something like this: "Hello. How are you? You have beautiful hair. C'est magnifique! Are you alone? I am a hairdresser. I am from Paris. Can I buy you a drink? I would love to fix your hair. You speak English? You are English, no?"

"No." I kept ignoring him, only answered in such a way that only the most rude blockhead could pursue me. I said I had to go since someone was waiting for me. He asked me if I had a boyfriend. I said, pointedly, yes. He asked to see a picture of my boyfriend. I was walking away from where I wanted to go, in an effort to escape him, and decided to go into a restaurant instead of further detouring. That was a mistake, as he followed and would not let me pay for my food; therefore I only got coffee, therefore he ordered food and then thrust it at me. He asked me if I would like some money. I am sitting looking disgusted and making nasty sarcastic

Continued on next page

Narrative II: A European Trip

Continued from previous page

"shutup" answers. He takes the clip out of my hair, puts his hand around my waist and under my blouse. He lowers his voice and leans closer, bites my ear and says, "Do you know what I really wish? I want to make love to you. I will do such things to your body you have never known. You will not believe what I will do." Such Gaulic charm. I am obviously not responding, and suddenly he thinks he has hit on the key: "I know—you are a— hee-pee. I should have know!" He is delighted to have hit on this discovery. "You want to *relate*. We will be meaningful. We will talk about peace, no? Do you march in Washington? We should love each other—everybody love, no? Deep down inside, I am a very sensitive person. . . ." Eventually I removed myself from him. I wonder if he gave me the finger as I walked away.

Darius Brun, our Besancon advisor, would not let me carry my suitcase from our train to the taxi. He had gone to Antioch many years before. He was prosperous, 35ish. Wife a psychological counselor; also more importantly a housewife and mother. Darius was super-French. Enthusiastic, talkative, determined to make us love Besancon as he did. He seldom spoke English but spoke slowly for me. He had a basic decency and prejudice for things French that was common to most of the older folk. He took Sara and me around to the ruins of old fortresses, pointed out walls standing from the Roman times, recounted tales of the city's history. One meal we had at his house stands out in my mind. Tastefully decorated apartment, good elaborate food. He invited me to toss the salad at the table, saying the test of a good woman was whether or not she could correctly toss a salad.

His wife bottlefed the baby at the table. His apparent great discontent in life was that he had two daughters, which was nice in itself, except it meant that so far there was no son to carry on his name. I spent much time in Besancon sitting in the park. It was spring, and the babies and pregnant women seemed as much in bloom as the flowers. I have never seen so many children as I did wheeled about the park in strollers. Sara and I loved the little stores and open markets—*pattiseries, boulangeries, charcuteries*. No credit to me, my best French phrase was *Je voudrais un comme ça*. We loved the public showers (only showers in Besancon?). We talked with local students, ate in their cafeteria (*couscous* and mackerel on end). With one French girl we went on a hike up the highest hill/ mountain in town. The lift that went up the mountain was broken so the French girl forged on up on foot. I envied her good physical condition— common to their youth—but thought she was crazy to make the hike in a skirt, hose, and high-heeled shoes.

Continued on next page

Narrative II: A European Trip

Continued from previous page

I loved the way the French had adopted Americanisms with their own flair to them. The small differences emphasized both the similarities and the gaps between the cultures. We shopped much at the *Uniprix,* the only "supermarket" in town; the similarity of convenience made us feel at ease. The fact that they sold bread unwrapped and used string bags instead of dispensing paper ones pointed up the enchanting difference. Having a bad cold I discovered all kinds of unique, mysterious preparations for real and imagined ailments (but no Contac).

Largely to get away from Sara I went to Nice by myself. I met three other American students—two who had spent a year in France and one who had been in Italy a year. We went to the Centre de Tourism in Nice where the multilingual staff provided free help to tourists in finding hotel reservations. However, it was the night before Easter, and every hotel in and around Nice was packed. We waited there, hoping someone would cancel hotel reservations, talking, smoking for five hours until the Centre closed at about 1 a.m. We were warned the police would chase us away if we slept on the beach, and trouped out in search of an all-night bar.

We discussed our adventures in Europe, the intercultural clashes, the views of America we had come across, the things we liked and didn't like about America in relation to Europe. By 4 o'clock we were considerably burnt-out sitting in the cold of a sidewalk cafe, guzzling coffee and beer by turns and wishing we had some amphetamines. At that point a Swede in an MG came by and asked, "You kids need a place to stay?" Our weariness overcame any sense of caution and we went with him to his apartment. It turned out that he was bringing us to his place primarily for revenge on his girlfriend; she was an American student who had the night before brought home three South Africans to stay in their cramped apartment, who were still there when we arrived.

I have a streak of social appropriateness in my nature, and was the only one of us students who managed to stay awake in his car as he drove along the Riviera from Nice to his place in Monaco. I nodded and mumbled "uh-huh, uh-huh" to his tour ("That's the Casino area . . . Back there, that's the Rolling Stone's new villa. . . ."). I was rewarded when the places for sleeping were parcelled out by being parcelled into bed with him (along with two others) and spent the night coping with his advances. I thought it a very mealy sort of thing for him to do, and was annoyed at the stupidity of it. I knew the stereotype of Swedes, and imagined the parade of stereotypes he must have of me. I wanted him to know that not every American woman student was a whore.

I decided I would let him try any sort of pursuasion or seductive

Continued on next page

Narrative II: A European Trip

Continued from previous page

technique he wished, but that I would not let him screw me and would not make any physical gesture to him. If he didn't understand what was happening, he could ask. I guess I didn't think he would though, and he didn't. Perhaps he thought I was a prude or frigid. He ended up beating off over me, about four hours later. A somewhat hollow triumph, or not one at all. But I was left with a sense of wonder by that whole night, at his complete misunderstanding. At all the things that happen without one word of interchange or explanation; at the assumptions about what is happening, unfounded. I never said a word to him about that, nor did he. We assumed certain things would happen, others did, and that was that.

It turned out, if I was to believe his American girlfriend, that the man was a worm. He was living off a woman who was at that moment in the hospital having a vital operation, and he wouldn't visit her. In fact, he was enjoying the use of her sweaters and jeans. The American girl wanted to go home, but he had stolen a hundred dollars from her suitcase and she couldn't afford the plane fare now.

That morning, sunny and pleasant, we got on the bus back to Nice, to find hotels and go our separate ways. The Felliniesque quality of the episode was enhanced by the first palm trees I had ever seen. There was a drunk old man in the back of the bus who had been to America once; he talked about how he was going to get rich from some investment and then go to the States and buy a ranch out West and be a cowboy. It was Easter morning.

A few hotel rooms were available, but we had to split up and take singles. I had a nap and unloaded my stuff, then went out to see what there was to see in Nice. Impulsively, that evening, I went back to the Centre de Tourism, went inside. There they were, students, families, chic couples, waiting for a room; all the hotels in Nice filled because of Easter; "You can wait until we close at 1:00 a.m., in case a reservation is cancelled." And the students were asking about sleeping on the beach. The earth slipped inside of me. The faces were tired and somewhat anxious, but the students were joking and smoking, and I was part of them and they were me. So I threw back my head and laughed. Then I looked and saw one guy fiddling with a pipe, sitting on the floor.

He was small, with long stringy brown hair that looked black from being dirty; wire-frame glasses, a greasy black leather jacket and black jeans and boots; but a fine, delicate face and soft gestures. I went to him and asked for a match. He looked as though he thought that was an odd thing for me to do, but being genteel he lit my cigarette. I asked what he was doing there and he indicated two girls and two other men with whom he

Continued on next page

Narrative II: A European Trip

Continued from previous page

was travelling. The girls were American high schoolers spending a year in England, he was a Londoner, and he and the other two men were "chaperoning" the girls on a French holiday. The girls were going by train, and the men had motorcycles. His name was Jay.

We talked about the hotel situation and I described our previous night at the Centre de Tourism, and speculated that he might expect the same thing. He asked me if I'd like some tea at the cafe, and we left the others there in case a room became available. The talk gained momentum as it went, instead of the reverse as usually happens. We spent most of the night talking. Let me tell you about Jay. He was different from me because he was British and I was American; and also because he was Jay and I was Sadiepat. What did we talk about? He had spent four years at Trinity College in New Hampshire, and liked the States. He had spent part of his childhood in France. I can only remember snatches now, but we talked until 3 or 4 in the morning . . .

About Alfred Jarre's play, *Ubu Roi,* for one thing. It was a preoccupation of his, as was all the absurd. And at length about Marcel Proust, *A la Recherche du Temps Perdu.* That was very much part of Jay. The beauty of life was in childhood, when we were awake to our senses and to wonder, when we understood and knew nothing, and so could feel. Now that we are old we are sometimes touched—we eat a piece of cake and are flooded with sensations and realize—ah, yes! I used to eat those cakes at tea at my aunt's, when I was a child. Then the door closes and we are old again, and dead. So all that is desirable is to wait, to stumble on that unexpected sensual cue to open the door on life again.

He fell in love with me, I think, because he felt I was a child beyond that door, and maybe I held it open for him. I was full of life, and he thought he was full of death. I had felt together with all those eager, tired people at the Centre de Tourism (people who might stumble into a Fellini adventure that night when all they wanted was a soft bed) and I had thrown back my head and laughed. When he saw me there laughing, he said later, he thought "You are in color, and all the rest are in black and white."

Of course he was not full of death; he was just full of beautiful words and ideas that sometimes had no anchor. I was an anchor. The metaphors don't mix—maybe one metaphor can't hold the complexity of it: I was a door into a child-world of ignorant sensualness; and I was an anchor to secure his floating abstractions down to the palpable earth.

I thought then that I fell in love with him because he was the one

Continued on next page

Narrative II: A European Trip

Continued from previous page

and only person I've ever met who made me want to talk, more and more. I never thought what I was to say next, nor paused vacantly with my mind wandering. My main inner conflict, the way I'd characterize myself in a book jacket, would be to say I have a force pulling me toward sleep, laziness, cynicism, fatness, and another toward growing, struggling, laughter. With Jay the conflict was totally resolved; I was awake. There was always some energy to share.

We talked about my past and his, about male/femaleness and being free. About relationships—group marriage, women's lib, French chauvinism. About Antioch and Trinity and British schools. Theater, theories of acting, the movie he was thinking of making with friends. The counterculture, books, movies, music.

Did I mention that by 4 a.m. I was in love? I don't use that phrase lightly. There are others I had related to more deeply but none for whom I'd had that all-they-ever-promised emotion. The fulfillment of childhood myths. I talked at length about David—

(I'd known David for years, hadn't liked him, fell in with him ambiguously, fought, changed with him. David was then a biting, cold son of a bitch. Unemotive, cynical and judgmental. Never opened doors or said "I like your dress" or lit my cigarette, at a time when I and most of America wanted if not expected these things for women. Would not be nice or tender or kind, or dishonest. So smart and sharp. I said, "he won't let me be weak; I can't lean on him, he won't give anything up for me; he won't give me what I sometimes want but shouldn't have because it would make me miserable in the long run—things like security. . . ." He had begun to soften a touch, while we were at different colleges, but his integrity never faded. . . .)

But Jay said things few American men ever could or would seriously say then. Like, "You were in color . . ." Later he said, bitterly, "I got you on the rebound from David—it's him you want." It was my American self-centered, ebullient naivety, my disregard for privacy and disrespect of boundaries that let me talk so about David. My relationship with David (whom I married later) was more solid, realistic, lasting—a kind of love I would have had to find with Jay. Because the love with Jay was, like joy, a peak and not a process.

I could describe it more—"romantic, exciting, excruciatingly bright, two people feeling like they had each happened onto the only other live person in the world"—but the phrases sound too familiar and thus belittling. If David was for me a door, Jay was a mirror . . .

Continued on next page

Narrative II: A European Trip

Continued from previous page

Jay was pessimistic. David snapped at people like a gleeful dog in a fight; Jay just winced, as he remarked on the world. . . . He had spent a week alone at a friend's house in California, sitting by the pool in the sun, smoking opium, floating—"Yeah, I could get hooked on that. I could see it," he said, and laughed painfully.

I talked about *Le Petit Prince;* it reminded me of the Proustian idea. The fox said, "I do not eat bread—the wheatfields are of no use to me. And that is sad. But you have hair the color of gold. It will be marvellous when you tame me! The wheat, which is gold, will remind me of you. And I will love the sound of the wind in the wheat. . . ." And when the prince had to leave the fox, and the fox cried, "J'y gagne, dit le renard, à cause de la coleur du ble."

It was important to me. His book—*Recherche du Temps Perdu*—a monumental work. I saw a BBC TV show on Proust in London. He spent the last—how many, 5 years?—of his life in bed searching for crumbs of cakes to bring back lost time, writing the book. *Le Petit Prince?*—a fable, a child's book. The European pool of age and history, Catholic mystery; the Americanness of youth, simplism. . . . Children mostly are not yet defeated, wrung out—

We talked until we couldn't keep awake any longer, went back to my room. They wouldn't let him stay, not because we were unmarried, but because it was a "single" and could not serve two, even if we paid for two. I took his pack and helmet and went to sleep while he and his friends slept on the beach, between bouts with the police who chased them away.

He came back that morning. We talked awhile and he wanted me to come to bed with him. I told him no, explained lengthily. I'd been to bed with many men over two years because I had no good reason to say no, and some good reasons to say yes. I'd asked nothing of them because I didn't want to use sex as a club. Had received not much love but much that was more valuable than love. But basically I'd spent two years hopping from one city to another, person to another, bed to another. Had some freedom, self-direction, variety, excitement, but had skimming, non-involvement, incompletion, rootlessness, shallowness too. I'd decided to say "no" to men sexually, until there was a real relationship, grown over time and days of talk and getting-to-know.

I would then be more free. Because in sex I also bound myself up, restricted myself, comme ça: "You can't ask for him to see only you, you can't be possessive, you can't ask him to touch you in public, to act like he loves you, you can't ask . . ." I expected them to give nothing because I wanted to be perfect, and the perfect woman asks nothing except what

Continued on next page

Narrative II: A European Trip

Continued from previous page

is most desirable—that is, creativity, challenge, honesty, instead of deadly, contemptible security or comfort. Illogically though, I had strong urges to give people what I thought they wanted, what they needed, like love, reassurance, support, and sex. I had given to men what my standard said I must, in order to be a successful person—sex, free unneurotic sex without manipulative, whorish demands. A perfect example of an unliberated woman made less free by women's liberation.

I knew that was fucked, I explained, and I was getting screwed, and I had had many lovers and few friends during my Antioch years. So, I told Jay, "No." He looked at me like he had at first—like he thought I was very strange; but being British, genteel, circumspect, respecting privacy and accepting differences in a way I did not, he just nodded and said "okay" with a quizzical smile. Got in bed, obviously exhausted, closed his eyes.

I got in bed and made love with him.

We left our respective groups, got on his cycle and rode down the coast, then cut through the hills, taking all the time in the world. Shaking cold, tired on the bike coming into Grasse, little town with a big perfume factory filling the air. Cycle on cobblestones, little hotel, lots of stairs, sometimes an ancient lift. Double beds, Jay's pipe and cherry tobacco on the old walnut table next to my passport and wallet. Restaurant, French bread, wine, fish, camembert cheese; a French lady feeding her tiny poodle, holding it in her lap at the restaurant. Cycle flying around the curbs, hills, villages with red roofs, Jay, enthralled, big bathtubs, brown rough toilet paper. Petit déjeuner—croissants and milky coffee, crumbs in the bed and Jay in the bed in the morning. Charcuteries, boulangeries, "Bonjour, madame," when we entered a store, "Bonjour, madame," when we left. We saw movies—commercials at the beginning, and awful travelogues. The laundromat, with French movie magazines, the children playing in the laundry baskets and shyly talking to us. The cycle, four hours in the shaking sun; we stop, still vibrating, have a single beer on empty stomachs and the world softens, yet lifts; everything blurred but each sensation magnified—sound of glasses clinking, smell of the bike we've carried in on our bodies, my back against the chair. . . .

His hair was dirty and matted because of riding the cycle, and he didn't care enough about his body to fuss with it. We washed it and I combed out the tangles. Long, bright brown hair, soft, living.

He had seemed shell-shocked when I met him. He'd had much bad luck with women (what man hasn't?). He said once, "I had managed to forget I had a body, until you reminded." He'd had an affair with a woman who was divorced; scene in the bedroom, her telling him about

Continued on next page

Narrative II: A European Trip

Continued from previous page

the husband, a brutal sort, growling, "Open your legs!" and "You're as dry as an artichoke!" and so she'd been afraid of sex. It was pathetic, intolerable, and very funny. His women seemed to have been that kind, sort of leftovers from Nathaniel West's *Miss Lonelyhearts*—unlovable people copulating and hating it but drawn by the mock-up of intimacy it provided. I suppose I was the first woman he'd made love to who enjoyed making love, and that made the relationship, the kind of love it was, all the more perfect.

What happened? Two perfect weeks. Then he put me on the train to Besancon, said he'd be there in a couple of weeks. I had to get back more quickly because my language class was due to start or some such, or maybe it was already happening, the pulling apart. What was the order? Don't know—these things happened:

He wanted to go back to the States but couldn't get a visa except possibly as an immigrant; but that would mean he'd end up in Viet Nam, not the States. My idea—a joke—a stroke of genius—marry me, stay British, but they'll let you come to the States. Then we'd get divorced. We lit up at the idea. Such a goof! Absurd! And for a while . . . we could pretend. . . . He said, "But the awful thing is, we might decide we *like* being married. Wouldn't that be *ghastly*? What would we do then?" And that melded pain and laughter in him.

He took so long to get to Besancon. A week? "I'm going to go to London," I told him in the cafe when he came (his hair matted again). I was supposed to be in a program of creative writing there anyway, after spending three months in France. I didn't want to become half-rooted in France, become part of it and then be ripped up with French earth still clinging to my roots, and tossed back to England, and then the States. I couldn't straddle two continents. . . . Besides, I didn't want to spend my time liberating Frenchmen, so that I could communicate with them intelligently, after I'd learned French better. . . . If Jay didn't want to live with me, okay, I said. I'm not possessive, I said. You're getting possessive, he said. You're attaching strings, he said. Looking irritated, but wounded like I'd destroyed something, and cynical like he knew it would be destroyed, had to be. From then on, I was no longer there for him.

The inside of my apartment in Besancon was 10° colder than outside because of the thick stone walls. Tall, a 14' or 16' ceiling so I always felt like a child in there. He made me cut off 6" of his hair. I had a miserable cold. Sara didn't approve of him much. He wouldn't make love to me, only argue. I tried once to seduce him just so that I could spurn him and say "There, fuck you, that's how I feel." But he didn't even realize what I was doing; he had turned himself off and would not notice my trying

Continued on next page

Narrative II: A European Trip

Continued from previous page

to seduce him. He said, "I loved you because you were so free, so independent. I had never known anyone so independent."

And, "Why do you want to go to *England?* It's wet and cold there." I went, nonetheless, by myself. I knew that even if what I said was untrue, it could become true. If he wanted me to be independent, I would make myself so. Besides—I knew I'd fall out of love with him and then get down to the sensible, practical business of working at the other kind of love, the kind that lasts. Once I'd lost the sense of his being perfect, being exactly right, I would naturally slip back to sanity and become a person who would no longer stand in the courtyard of the apartment waiting for him to come. I knew he was a good person with beautiful elements in him, as was I. All we had to do was cash in these principles, these guises like "You're independent" or decisions, "You love me too much." But he talked and fell in love with words.

Okay, I'll give it to him, damn it—I was clinging to him. You could probably see the marks of my fingernails on him. True. But no more true than—"You were in color and the rest were in black and white." Which is, of course, a ridiculous statement. Is poetry, not reality. Europe is like that, poetry, abstraction. America is . . . concrete.

He was gone sour again. I said something once about nothing being permanent, life changing, and he said, "Yes, but sometimes it just seems to go *on* and *on*. . . ."

He'd talked about Nabokov's *Lolita,* and when I was in London I read it. I enjoyed it but didn't understand why someone would want to make love with a 13-year-old. One of the few times I saw Jay in London he took me to a park, and finding nothing to say to me he watched the kids —6-to-10-year-olds, playing. He said, "Aren't they beautiful? They're so innocent," he said, half-seriously, half-wickedly. Innocent, full of life, full of themselves, and I guess an old man could go crazy wanting to grab some of that for himself. I thought then I understood *Lolita.*

Going to London, I knew Jay might not get there for several days, or perhaps not at all. I looked up a girl I had known at Antioch and found her apartment in a run-down part of London that looked much like Richmond. She wasn't there, but a nun in street clothing took me into a room to wait for her; there were childish scrawls and murals on the walls, pillows but no furniture, and a couple of scraggly kittens. I went into the bathroom and passed by a disheveled man reciting a speech from *Moby Dick* and acting as though he were freaking out on acid. Strange howls of laughter and bits of conversation and music floated about and I felt pretty much at home.

Continued on next page

Narrative II: A European Trip

Continued from previous page

When my friend got there she hustled me out for a long walk, and explained that she was glad to see me but I could not crash at her place, because the people living there got upset when new people passed through. It turned out to be a house filled with drop-outs, students and schizophrenics. It had been started by R.D. Laing, the Englishman who believes that psychotics can best adjust by living with sympathetic "sane" people in the regular community. I left the place feeling strangely at home with the absurdity and craziness I'd come across; but disgruntled without a place to stay.

I stayed for a few days in a tourist house (complete with raw bacon for breakfast, with people on a planned vacation plan) and then settled into a hostel, which was empty because of the season. I went to a few museums, but mainly stayed away from the tourist route. I watched a lot of BBC TV, from the Prime Minister talking about politics and impressing me with how politically culture-centric I am to a documentary on aging and the aged to a series on Elizabeth I that was later imported to the States. I watched the "May Day Demonstrations" on TV, the ones in Washington where the demonstrators blocked the streets into the city and were arrested wholesale, illegally. I reflected that my father was probably prevented from going to work, and wondered if David was there in the crowds. It was a time spent reflecting at a distance on my country, its young people and their parents also.

I also saw James Taylor and Neil Young, superstars on the rock scene, for the first time on BBC. They had wonderful half hours of sitting and playing by themselves on a small stage before a small audience. It was like the British, to take the cultural and musical events that the stars were and to put them in a tasteful, warm and subdued setting where their music could be enjoyed without the hysteria of an American rock concert. At the Neil Young showing there were two Canadian boys watching with me. Young had on ragged jeans and a flannel shirt, and one of the Canadians remarked deprecatingly, "He sure got into his Sunday best clothes for this." I thought how little even some Canadians understood or were part of the American counterculture. It was especially ironic because Neil Young is Canadian.

I read *Alice in Wonderland,* T.S. Eliot and also e.e. cummings. ("whatever we lose like a you or a me, it's always ourselves we find in the sea". . . .) I also bought *Dune* because David had recommended it, but lost it in the subway, but hoped some English person would find it and be exposed to American science fiction, and a mute transaction would have taken place between us. I didn't go into the pubs much because I was

Continued on next page

Narrative II: A European Trip

Continued from previous page

intimidated by drinkers, and thought that if anywhere in England English men would put aside their reserve enough to try and pick me up, it would be there. But the few times I did go in a pub, the TV was always turned to American shows, of the *I Spy* and *Star Trek* genre. The closest I ever got to being picked up by an Englishman was when I gently turned down a ragged old man who was obviously very lonely and had a long talk with me, and offered to find me a job and let me stay at his flat.

I met a very friendly, attractive Irishman who someone told me had been a promising track star in Ireland, and who told me where in St. James one could buy grass, but I never checked to see how reliable he was. I spent a week looking for a flat and a job. I had no work permit, of course, but no questions were asked when I found an agency that needed temporary typists. They sent me out to a Tea Import Export company. I spent a week there, typing a form letter to English people who had saved their "Match for Cash" coupons and sent them into the Tea contest. The mail workers and others had been on strike and I had to address the form letter telling them to be patient and they would have their chance for a free vacation, or whatever the prize was, when the mail had caught up. Their were two workers there very representative of the attitudes toward Americans.

Both were very attracted to America, one loving it and the other hating it. One was a lovely girl, soft and gentle, taking me to lunch and expertly keeping me doing the talking, wishing she could visit America. The kind of cultured, soft-voiced girl that American businessmen wanted for secretaries, instead of the gossiping, smoking, eating-at-their-desks, poor-spelling girls they tended to be stuck with, at least in Washington. She was one dainty feminine pillow. The other had the same graces, only undercut with a bitterness. She asked if I had no other dress, one with a short skirt instead of my floor-length one, and if all girls in the States went without bras. She dismissed America, saying she would hate to live there because it was all too fast, tense and demanding. I would find, she said, that they did things at a more relaxed, enjoyable pace.

In fact, the letters I had to get out were not noticably slow-paced as they were piled onto my desk. It was not much different from all the corporate offices I'd worked at on temporary jobs in America. One difference though: there was a large lounge with stuffed couches and a refrigerator, filled with all kinds of soft and hard beverages to refresh visitors. I'd never seen a spread like that except at special occasions in Washington offices. But it was for the executives and their visitors only. It seemed a little like

Continued on next page

Narrative II: A European Trip

Continued from previous page

the English hospitality and genteelness were kept on show, but American hustling business practices were undershoring them. America was the axis of the world; perhaps because in the 20th century Americans have thought it so, except in their daydreams of a vacation plan including Merrie old England and the Louvre of Marie Antoinette. That was the source of some of the bitterness.

Jay took me on a motorcycle tour thirty miles away from London, and we stopped for a Coke in a Woolworth-like store. He had been complaining because the roads were so inferior to America's. We passed settlement after settlement of condominiums and apartment houses crushed together, looking like the early Washington suburbs thrown up in the 1950's. There were too damn many people crammed into these small islands, he said; and maybe he would, after all, someday move to the States.

I was scheduled to go into a Creative Writing workshop, lasting a semester in London, but my Antiochian friend had told me that the man who taught it was far over the hill. He was so hard of hearing that he would cock his head when you spoke, and then answer you with something completely unrelated to your comment, something probably reminiscent of Antioch twenty years ago, or creative writers of the 1940's. I had learned a great deal, at an accelerated pace in Europe, and I knew I would be right in going home. I later found this comment in a book called *At the Edge of History:*

> As I brooded over the Irish Revolution and Watts, I became aware of the irony that I had moved away from California to look for real and historically deep cultures at a time when California's turn to make history had come. . . . I had been offered an Old Dominion Fellowship, supposedly to work in London, but I told myself that it was silly to labor on some piece of academic criticism at a time when history was becoming possessed with visions of an angelic and diabolic kind. America in the winter of 1966–67 seemed to be in the beginning of some huge transformation, and Ronald Reagan and the hippies were a joint persuasion that a new exchange between myth and history was taking place at the edge of history.

It was 1971, a far cry from 1967, and in some ways the counterculture had experienced what England went through over centuries: a triumphing of self and of culture, a belief that the sun would never set on one's own

Continued on next page

Narrative II: A European Trip

Continued from previous page

unique and great civilization, and then a witnessing of that culture's disintegration and even humiliation before a greater, self-infatuated and uncontrollable civilization. There were threads remaining, perhaps the most important and beautiful ones, but they were enmeshed in a chaos of obscuring frayed warp and woof. Beyond that, my travels had begun to make me feel where my roots were, and I learned that I was not completely an international citizen, a neutered person without a culture, without a home.

I wanted to protect my parents from the part of me they were hurt by; and the main means to that, I thought, was financial independence, so I decided to quit Antioch, which was quite expensive, and find a job. I wanted to complete my encounter with David. The emotional spree with Jay was over, and I was going home.

One of the few things I did with Jay when he got to London was to go to the British National Museum where there was a special exhibit of the painting which has been familiarized to Americans by an insurance ad. It was a Dutch painting showing a marriage, the couple surrounded by medieval symbols of marriage, love, religion and such. I sat in Trafalgar Square waiting for Jay; and I was meditating among the pigeons, somewhat self-consciousness since children coming by kept squealing, "Look, that girl's meditating!" and then whispering and giggling. After Jay arrived we rushed into the museum and waited impatiently as the line of tourists filed past the painting. Jay squinted at it once and said, "Look— my friend told me! You can see the artist there in the picture, reflected in the mirror. He painted himself in." I could not see it, but took him on his word; and then he rushed me out. Like David, he had little patience for long meditations on art.

A selection from *On the Edge of History*. A young history professor, in 1966, has been visiting Esalen and trying to understand and absorb this new counterculture and its impact on his beloved and comprehensible knowledge of history. He is watching a frenzied "hippie" in a drugged trance dance naked and scream before a camp fire:

> It was one thing to celebrate, following R. D. Laing, the schizophrenic as the culture hero of an alienated society, and it was quite another thing to stare unperturbed into the violent eyes of a person who has gone out of his mind. Ira said that once you have gone out of your own mind you know how to handle other people who go out there too, but the direction in which this

Continued on next page

Narrative II: A European Trip

Continued from previous page

> bare-chested fire worshiper was moving was not the same one that attracted me. I had had enough of the whole conjuration, but I knew that in leaving I was only proving the broader humanity that Ira practiced beyond my limitations. I could not attend on freaks with loving care. The underside of Esalen was exposed and I felt uneasy, sensing it was I who was really being exposed.

In a sense my whole first two years at Antioch was a preparation for my European trip, since I knew from the start that I would be going abroad. It seems necessary in our modern culture to be able to adapt successfully to rapidly changing times. My parents were not adept at this, and a large part of the pain in their lives has come from this dependence on permanence. Antioch was a two-year crash course in how to depend on myself and how to maintain a sense of self when the psychological supports in my life were lost. My expectancy and acceptance of change shaped my European experience. However, both of the experiences (Antioch and Europe) brought me to understand that the connections between things, the maintenance of what is worthwhile over time are something I need. I know that, to be adaptable, one does not have to continually destroy what one has. As the *I Ching* says, there are limits even to limitation; and the modern American characteristic of transiency—of always changing one's life-style and affiliations—is in itself a rigid form of bondage.

Since I returned from Europe I have formed some more lasting attachments. I believe in and maintain, for instance, my very good relationship with my husband, my pleasure and satisfaction in writing, and my self-acceptance. I am not afraid of change and of losing what I value because experientially I have learned that my *ability* to find happiness survives change. I also have learned not to throw away that which I value just because I am afraid that if I do not cast it off, it will cast me off. The experience of cultural change has taught me not to fear what I may lose, but to be happy with what I have and open to what I may gain.

Chapter V

⅋⅋⅋⅋⅋⅋

Assessment and Award of Credit

By now it is probably obvious that the process of granting credit for prior learning is clearly one of assessment and evaluation. Again, we are talking about an examination procedure which has definable criteria and instruments. The criteria dictate what composes the student's portfolio and how that material is organized; the instruments dictate how the assembled material is examined.

In the faculty-based model of assessing prior learning the faculty, students, and the interchange between them constitute the principal instruments of evaluation. Faculty, having been involved from the beginning in determining what shall be credited and what constitutes proper and sufficient documentation, are the architects of the process as well as the instruments of implementation. While faculty have available to them some measures created by others, the majority of instruments must be constructed to fit each student and his/her particular situation. The creativity required is a challenge recognized by many faculty who have been involved. It can be likened to the inventiveness needed to construct a course or other future learning event. And, like many creative acts, it may be accompanied by some discomfort. The pain, however, should be truly the pain of creativity and not of confusion or frustration.

Unfortunately, faculty reveal that the various methodologies they must use are causing significant confusion and frustration. Most of this can be traced back to the fact that, at the beginning, the entire process has not been thought through thoroughly enough. In some programs students are sent to faculty members with no more instruction than "See how many credits this trip to Europe is worth," or "Mr. X has run his own business for ten years. How many credits can we give him for that?" While others are told that all life/work experience must fit into course equivalences and, therefore, whatever measures are used in the classroom should be used for assessing prior learning.

Those that have managed to survive some of these early traumas have developed evaluation techniques which are both legitimate to the discipline and relevant to the student. As has been mentioned before, no one feels that he/she has the perfect —or even near perfect—methodology. Time and experience provide a level of ease which makes it possible for interested faculty to experiment and find methodologies comfortable for them and the students.

Criteria

The establishment of clear and mutually understood criteria is essential for constructing methods which accurately assess prior learning. Whatever the discipline, students, colleagues, administrators, and third parties must be able to agree on not only (1) what is to be credited and (2) how that which is to be credited is to be assembled, but (3) what techniques will be used to assess the various learnings, skills, and competences. Most programs agree that there can be prior agreement on what is to be credited and how the material is to be assembled. While few actually had accomplished this by the time they began the process, at least there was agreement that it would be wise to do so. Few programs, however, see the need for an a priori identification of techniques and methodologies. As a matter of fact, many see a distinct advantage in allowing the techniques, processes, and methodologies to evolve over a period of time through actual case situations.

One administrator puts it this way, "I think the guidelines should be developed from experience rather than arbitrarily preceding experience; . . . there should be a series of guidelines which reflect the methodologies of assessment in the various disciplines. It seems to me that you cannot measure the knowledge base in Russian literature in the same way that you measure the skills of a teacher."

While there are obvious differences among disciplines, of course, these need not prevent some prior agreement on methodology, just as these differences do not negate consensus on what is to be credited. And the fact that the crediting process is highly individualized does not remove the need for some common understanding of appropriate assessment techniques. The criteria for choosing particular techniques are just as important as those for selecting content. "Shall we use written or oral examinations?" "How many years of work equal so many credits?" "Shall we have the student demonstrate interviewing techniques before a panel of experts of our choosing, or shall we take the word of an unknown third party?" These are typical criterion-referenced questions. They do *not* dictate specific methods but they do lead to a commonly understood criteria.

Trust and Student Input

These questions, and the many others like them, raised at the outset allow students and faculty to build the trust which is essential to the process. Students feel a definite need and desire to be involved in establishing the parameters of evaluation techniques as well as content. It is somewhat surprising to find that students want a part not only in what is to be credited but also in how their knowledge, skills, and competences will be examined. When given the choice, for example, some students prefer oral to written exams. Some students definitely believe that third-party evaluation alone will not do them justice. These students want faculty to test their competences and skills.

One student voiced considerable frustration when asked what part she played in the crediting of her prior learning. "They asked me to describe what I had learned from leading groups in a drug rehabilitation program. When I asked if they meant what theory I had learned or what I was able to actually do with the kids, I was told that they wanted both. The theory I could put on paper—the other, even though I had references from my co-leaders, I would have had to show them. But there was no provision for this. Even though I got the credit, I would have been happier had I been able to show what I could do."

The trust factor between students and faculty members in a process as new as crediting prior learning is not to be taken lightly. Since no one is yet—or is likely to be in the very near future—expert in the various methodologies involved, faculty need student input so that all facets of previous learning can be explored. The student narrative, the major vehicle for conveying content in the faculty-based model, is an unusual and sensitive document which can reflect what both the student and the faculty desire only if there is trust. How that writing is to be examined *and by whom* need to be settled before the student commits one word to paper. This agreement usually is reached during preliminary counseling or prior learning assessment workshops where students and faculty have opportunities to exchange ideas and discuss the students' total programs. Clearly delineated assessment techniques certainly will move the entire process ahead with less confusion and resentment.

The Narrative

Since the student narrative is the primary document to be evaluated in so many programs, it deserves a central focus in any discussion of assessment techniques. Faculty identify the evaluation of the narrative as one of the most troublesome aspects of the entire process. Unlike a term paper, which usually feeds back a predetermined body of knowledge, the narrative covers material with which the faculty member has had little or no previous contact. Even if faculty and students have talked over criteria and parameters, the knowledge base conveyed in the narrative is the student's, and faculty must deal with it on its terms and decide how well knowledge is conveyed.

No one technique will service the narrative. What is culled out, dissected, approved, and credited will be determined by the faculty member's own experience and his/her discipline. A careful examination of the policeman's narrative presented at the end of Chapter Four illustrates this point. If this narrative were presented to faculty from the disciplines of criminal justice, sociology, and psychology, varying decisions on the scope and depth of learning, understanding, and the ability to communicate what was learned most certainly would be reached. Furthermore, such subjective factors as the faculty member's experience or lack of it in similar situations would also influence the decision. Taken as a whole, this narrative demonstrates great sensitivity and personal growth. But these are rather vague and general conclusions not easily translatable into credits. Perhaps if this student had been coached to identify definite psychological or sociological theory, the granting of credit would be less difficult. But then one runs the danger of overstructuring and thereby limiting what the student identifies as his learning.

One of the ways out of these troubled waters is to combine the narrative with an oral examination. This exam might sound dangerously like a doctoral dissertation defense, but conducted in the spirit of trust and partnership in learning mentioned earlier, it turns out to be a most useful learning device for the student. This entire process *does* occur early enough in the student's total education program so that it is not a life or death affair. The oral examination is also an effective way of helping the student identify strengths and weaknesses in thought and expression, identification which can be extremely useful in structuring future learning events. If conveyed as a nonthreatening learning experience, the oral exam can succeed. If presented as an instrument of medieval torture, it will fail.

Many programs do not allow student and examiner to meet. The entire portfolio is given to either one faculty member or a committee, and the deliberations are held without the student's physical presence. The argument for this procedure is that it adds immensely to the objectivity of the deliberations. This is undoubtedly true. But not allowing the student to participate at this crucial point also robs the examiners of immediate input which is often crucial to the evaluation. One administrator opposed to this method said, "We want to spare the faculty and students the undignified embarrassment of a horse-trading session." Almost all faculty and administrators report that once students gain confidence, they do wish to negotiate. This practice, of course, is not uncommon among *all* students, whether the negotiating be for prior learning credits, the grade received on a paper, or the amount of work required in a particular course. Involving students at every step including the evaluation session often consumes less time and energy than going through a lengthy appeal process.

The pejorative reference to *horse-trading* by the administrator in question demonstrates a basic mistrust of the integrity of both faculty and students. Most faculty and administrators report that, while somewhat confusing at first, the methodologies developed with the help of student input work to everyone's satisfaction. Students also report a willingness and in quite a few instances an eagerness to be examined. The confidence built during the counseling sessions makes the students eager to demonstrate what they know and can do in a manner acceptable to faculty and student alike.

Evaluation by Committee

There seems to be a growing feeling that there is not only safety in numbers but also greater reliability. Therefore, committee assessment is coming into much greater use than the one-for-one examining technique. Programs which began by assigning the evaluation task to one faculty member are moving toward the committee, some because of the charge of "horse-trading," others because the particular prior learning events lend themselves more easily to a committee evaluation.

More than one reviewer should participate in translating a student narrative into academic credit, especially if it contains content from more than one discipline. Thus, it would be quite legitimate to review the narrative quoted in the preceding chapter for knowledge of intercultural understanding, knowledge of the dynamics of interpersonal relationships, and creative writing ability. Faculty from each of these areas would read the narrative and make judgments according to their field. It would be helpful, also, for more than one member from each discipline to evaluate the narrative because faculty from the same field probably would not judge the content of something so subjective in the same manner. Consensus among members of the same discipline is the desirable outcome. While many argue that the committee practice is cumbersome and costly, it *is* vital if the crediting process is to gain the respectability it deserves. Again, these decisions are among the first that need to be made if the process is to succeed.

As troublesome as the narrative may appear to a single evaluator, the competences and skills gained through work experience pose even greater problems. Though a faculty may decide in a most arbitrary, a priori fashion that one year of work on a particular job is worth twelve credits, this mechanism does little to evaluate what the student has learned from that job or what he/she is capable of doing. Those programs interested in having the student identify the learning and skills gained from working have found it necessary to evaluate these by means of a panel of experts. The panel is often comprised of people from the community who are knowledgeable in that particular field as well as a faculty person. This method differs significantly from the third-party evaluation already discussed in that it is assessing demonstrated abilities in the present and is under the direct supervision of the faculty. This method does not rely on letters of reference or supervisors' evaluations, regardless of how recent these might be.

The success of committees in evaluating work experience, student narratives, or other documented experiences depends to a large extent on their composition. The committee must be large enough to represent the various kinds of knowledge and competences presented by the student and yet small enough to be able to make effective decisions. The core of the committee should be composed of faculty whose expertise comes closest to the areas represented in the student's portfolio.

Students who have gone through the process should also serve as regular voting members of the committee. Although the practice of having students serve on evaluating committees is still extremely rare, those interviewed stated that they would welcome such an opportunity. The contributions of these participants would be great since many have backgrounds similar to those of students being evaluated. In addition, perspective on an evaluation committee adds to the trust as well as the growing partnership in learning between faculty and adult students who have prior learning.

Outside consultants usually are asked to serve on the committee as their expertise is needed, but in many programs they have no vote. Some professional programs that make heavy use of adjunct faculty members use one of these as the outside expert. In such a situation, the adjunct person does vote.

Some programs and institutions have found that rotating faculty members on an evaluation committee is beneficial. There is the danger of becoming routinized if committee membership is not changed. Often methods become fixed and standardized in the hands of faculty who remain on a committee for any length of time. This is especially true at the departmental and divisional level where faculty tend to deal constantly with the same or similar life/work experiences. The obvious need for continuity dictates a rotating committee whose members serve staggered terms. The rotation of committee members also has the advantage of introducing an ever-widening circle of faculty to the process, an important consideration in large departments servicing a special program. There is also growing evidence that as more faculty become involved, the special crediting process is more likely to be introduced into the regular program.

Amount of Credit

More often than not, consensus is reached on granting credit, but achieving agreement on how much to award is the toughest issue and one which has no ready solution. Without clearcut performance or competence objectives it is difficult to assign a definite number of credits without the usual time frame of the classroom. While it seems to be a relatively comfortable task to certify that a student has learned something, the quantification of that learning into credit units poses a major problem.

Regardless of the methodology employed, faculty are singularly unhappy with what they consider to be a "numbers game" within a process that bears no relation to the usual accumulation of credits. The only readily available guide is the class (course) equivalent. If learnings can be categorized and measured in terms of one or a combination of course equivalents, or grouped in disciplinary areas according to beginning, intermediate, and advanced levels, then the amount of credit to be granted is based on existing standards.

The direct translation of work experience into credit is handled in much the same way. In some programs the *number* of years employed becomes the *number* of credits to be awarded. Thus, a person who has worked successfully for three years as an accountant and has a letter from an employer verifying this automatically receives 12 semester hours of accounting (4 semester hours for every year worked). Whether this experience will be considered as beginning, intermediate, or advanced depends on the third-party evaluation and the description of duties. Obviously, every program puts a limit on the number of credits to be achieved in this manner. A person who has worked for twenty-five years as an accountant cannot receive 100 semester hours of credit in accounting!

Special adult programs which have to rely on a department-by-department evaluation of prior learning have considerably more trouble in determining the amount of credit to be awarded than do programs which see prior learning as the already completed portion of the student's total program. When an entire institution (Empire State College and Minnesota Metropolitan State College, for example) is devoted to building individual student programs, departmental and divisional vested interests are kept to a minimum because these units do not exist.

It *is* possible to arrive at the amount of credit to be awarded for prior learning in all programs. The reason this determination is seen as so difficult is that the current system of awarding credit is based on exposure—the amount of time spent in a classroom—rather than on the knowledge and skills gained. Faculty find it most difficult to *equate* what students have learned on their own with what they supposedly are learning within the framework of clock hours spent in a classroom, a laboratory, or supervised field experience. For now, calculation of exposure is the most efficient way to begin. Time spent in an accepted educational context is mutually understood by faculty, students, administrators, graduate schools, and even employers. Most institutions do not subscribe, as yet, to a competence- or performance-based curriculum, and until this is instituted, the semester hour *is* the clock hour.

It is imperative that everyone understands the amount of credit to be awarded at the outset. If crediting is to be done by seeking course equivalences, then the formula must be discussed and agreed on at the same time as the other basic questions are decided. Too many programs are unwilling to face this issue at the start because it is problematic and because individual faculty members are reluctant to commit themselves because of their insecurities with the process. Beginning with a course-equivalence formula will lessen this resistance and will allow faculty to move on to more creative ways of deciding the amount of credit to be awarded.

Student Appeals

While all programs claim that students may appeal the decision of a faculty evaluator or a committee, the formalization of this procedure is not widespread. This aspect demands much more attention than it has received. Students must have the right to appeal at least once. To deny the possibility of appeal is to state that the methods of awarding credit for prior learning are "fail-safe." As has been demonstrated, nothing is further from the truth. The appeal should be handled by a different committee and often introduces new or more detailed material. The only programs that have had significant appeals, interestingly enough, are those which began by using one-on-one evaluation rather than committee assessment.

Chapter VI

☆☆☆☆☆☆

Guidelines and Recommendations

It must be obvious by now that the state of the art of assessing prior learning is like the three-year-old child who can raise more questions than anyone can possibly answer. A few questions can be answered only at the national and regional levels, others are addressed to institutions, and some must be tackled by each faculty member, administrator, and student: questions of content, process, cost, reliability, validity, and what constitutes learning. The preceding pages have raised these issues and attempted some solutions. Continued activity in this area over the next few years certainly will raise more questions and suggest more answers.

In this chapter I suggest some actions to be carried out at the national and regional levels and some specific guidelines for institutions either contemplating the process or already involved.

Institutional Guidelines

Institutions about to try out awarding credit for prior learning and those already participating ask repeatedly for some rules. Indeed, what is usually requested is an ideal model. Like most of us, they would like the security of a precedent to follow. But, clearly, there is no one ideal model. As has been shown, practices vary from institution to institution and even from unit to unit within the same college or university. In many instances practices change from student to student because of the highly individualized nature of the process. So what are presented here are guidelines basic to any institutional deliberation and a framework on which specific practices can be built— a set of parameters that will allow faculty, students, and administrators to build cooperatively the crediting methods which make sense for their particular context.

1. *The decision must be made that crediting prior learning is legitimate and worth doing.*

The faculty-student body responsible for curriculum decides that crediting prior learning shall be instituted. This committee thinks through the principles of the process, establishes a sound academic rationale, and demonstrates a need among an existing student population or a new identifiable population. The rationale should include precedents from similar institutions or programs already involved as well as a preliminary description of possible procedures to be used.

2. *The decision to grant credit for prior learning must be widely disseminated and discussed.*

Contrary to the opinion of some, the "back door" method is not the most desirable. Though it might serve the purpose of immediacy, acceptance of the crediting practice as legitimate is hampered greatly by this approach. The discussions of the principles and parameters set by the faculty-student curriculum committee must include as many people as possible, especially the decision makers of the institution. While it is true that the process is a curriculum matter and thus the traditional province of faculty and students, there are matters of policy such as cost, acceptance of the credits by other institutions, and community assistance which affect the entire institution.

These open discussions must not be rushed even if this pace means postponing implementation for some months. The more the apparent and real resistance can be dealt with in these first discussions, the smoother the process will operate. The time spent is well worth the end results.

3. *The proper institutionwide policy-making group should vote to begin the crediting of prior learning.*

Once the curriculum committee is convinced that sufficient discussion has taken place, the process is brought before the larger institutional policy-making group for an affirmative vote. This body votes on the *principles and parameters* of the practice and charges the curriculum committee to establish specific criteria and procedures. At this point the curriculum committee can choose to work on the specifics themselves or delegate the responsibility to a special subcommittee.

4. *The committee to operationalize the process must represent the various interests concerned.*

The composition of this committee needs to be small enough to work effectively, yet large enough to include the variety of interests and expertise needed for effective implementation. If including all these interests forces the size of the committee to become unmanageable, then subcommittees oriented toward specific tasks must be organized. Included in this committee should be faculty, students, support staff—such as counselors, registrar, and admissions people—psychometrists, and selected representatives of the community. This latter group is especially helpful in working through some of the problems of third-party validation. The committee can disband once the process is under way, or it can continue, to act as a control and to work on new and expanded procedures.

5. *Decisions must be made as to exactly what is to be credited, when the crediting is to be accomplished, and whether or not prior learning needs to be related to future goals.*

These vital questions must be answered before any students are evaluated. They take time and effort to settle since they involve the fundamental educational philosophy of the total program as well as the crediting of prior learning. Beginning the practice before knowing and being able to communicate what is creditable life/work experience causes an intense anxiety and confusion among students and faculty. It also leads to the kind of mistrust which is extremely difficult to overcome at a later date. Programs and institutions which began before these questions had been discussed and answered attested to my statements here and acknowledged that the mistake, at best, was most difficult to correct. Not only do these questions logically precede the crediting process but, perhaps more importantly, they go a long way toward clarifying the total educational program for faculty and students.

6. *Decisions must be made about what it will cost the student and the institution, how supporting revenue can be raised, and whether or not faculty will receive remuneration for their efforts.*

Fiscal accountability and responsibility must be determined at the start. Although accurate cost data currently are scarce, institutions must come to grips with the fact that there are costs and that they must be handled responsibly. While it will take some actual experience to arrive at accurate figures, a flexible system of fees, other revenues, and compensation for faculty and outside examiners must be arrived at before the process begins.

The question of faculty remuneration either by payment or by released time is important to settle at the outset, especially in those special adult programs which use regular faculty to do the assessment. It is not an issue in those learner-as-central institutions where the evaluation of prior learning is integral to the faculty mentor's function.

7. *A decision must be made that faculty will receive recognition through the usual reward systems of promotion and tenure for their efforts in assessing prior learning.*

Unless administrators and other faculty recognize the value of the process and reward it in the same manner as the usual activities of classroom teaching, research, and publication, faculty will be hesitant to become involved. If faculty are not so rewarded, the procedure also is cast in a dubious light and not taken as seriously by the rest of the campus community as the traditionally rewarded activities.

8. *Proper application forms must be constructed as must clear, concise descriptive materials to be sent with them.*

The initial material received by the prospective student should contain sufficient information to give him or her an understandable overview of what is creditable and how the examination of prior learning will take place. Of course, this introductory information cannot be all-inclusive but it must be accurate and describe, with some typical examples, how the institution views the philosophical and operational aspects of crediting prior learning.

9. *Proper internal records and transcripts must be constructed to reflect adequately what has been credited and by what method the crediting has been carried out.*

This step requires some hard decisions on exactly what documentation needs to be kept, and for how long, to satisfy internal recordkeeping policies. In addition, transcripts which accurately reflect what has been credited, and how, must be constructed. The transcript, a document to convey what has been learned to either prospective employers or other institutions, is especially problematic with a process as new as crediting prior learning. While some institutions have elected to disguise the fact that certain credits were achieved through the evaluation of previous learning, this maneuver merely sidesteps an issue which must be faced sooner or later. If an institution believes in the process, then it must put forth the effort to describe its results openly to others. Not doing so tends to make a mockery of the entire practice.

Standard, computerized transcripts do not lend themselves easily to these new crediting procedures. While some institutions have had limited success with the computerized transcript, others have elected to become involved in the somewhat more cumbersome but infinitely more accurate narrative transcript. This type is preferable because it describes much more accurately what has been learned and how that learning has been documented, examined, and verified.

10. *A counseling system must be built which contains a prior learning assessment seminar and clearly takes a student-advocate approach.*

During the initial stage of the process students must have available a person who can help them translate experience into acceptable academic learning. This person must not be an advocate of the discipline to be examined or the future examiner, but someone who helps the student think through life/work experiences and compose them into statements of learning. This person must be supportive and understand that many students have a tendency to underestimate the academic worth of many of their experiences.

An additional counseling device is the semester-long, usually credit-bearing seminar which teaches students the art of portfolio preparation, especially that portion known as the student narrative. It also teaches students how to cull out learning from experiences and how other students view their particular experiences. Portfolio quality is appreciably better among students who participate in the seminars than among those who do not. Where possible, these classes should be run by counselors who can apply their student-advocacy role here as well.

11. *Clear, concise criteria must be established for the material the student is to include in the portfolio.*

The portfolio, consisting of all documented evidence required to evaluate prior learning, ranges from the extremely personal student narrative of experiences and learning to objective data such as transfer credits, standard national examination results, and third-party validation and corroboration. Each document included must have a reason for being there which is clearly understood by the student and the members of the committee who evaluate the portfolio.

It is important to make sure that third parties who are asked to validate or corroborate an experience understand exactly what is expected of them. Third parties usually do not participate in the initial planning group and therefore need quite explicit instructions on what their statements should contain.

12. *Explicit guidelines must be drawn up for the methodologies used to examine all the data in the portfolio.*

The way transfer credits are treated, what percentiles are acceptable from standardized national exams, and how third-party evaluations will be measured must be determined. Specific criteria will be agreed on for the student narrative, the central document to be evaluated in many programs.

All methodologies will be criterion-referenced. Students will know whether they are to be examined orally, by written statements, by demonstration of skills or competences, or by direct assessment of products such as paintings or other pieces of handiwork.

13. *Examination should be by committee rather than by only one faculty member.*

The dangers in the one-to-one evaluation method can be avoided easily by placing the decision in the hands of a committee. Personal biases are kept to a minimum as is the "horse-trading" practice sometimes found in the one-to-one situation. Committees should include faculty, students who have gone through the process, and outside experts when the occasion demands. Committee members, especially faculty, should be rotated so that a maximum number of people can participate. Rotation of committee members also prevents the process from becoming mechanized or routinized.

14. *Students must have the right to appeal the committee's decision.*

Appeal should be allowed only once and within a reasonable period of time. It is highly desirable for the appeal to be heard by a committee different from the one which made the original evaluation.

It is well to remember that these guidelines are just that. Some will not apply to certain institutions and programs; some may be too broad, others too narrow. But hopefully they will be useful and not restricting. In the final analysis, only the creative efforts of faculty, students, and administrators working with them, accepting them, rejecting them, modifying them will make these suggestions come alive.

Regional and National Concerns

A need exists for one national education agency to begin to establish broad philosophical and operational directions. As has been mentioned, it is up to the faculty and student body responsible for curriculum to establish specific techniques and to decide exactly what shall be credited. The programs and institutions I contacted agree that specifics are either institutional, programatic, divisional, or departmental prerogatives. At the same time, all are most anxious to have some nationally recognized organization issue the type of broad guidelines which would establish parameters and offer national approval of the basic concept. At this time the American Council on Education's Office on Educational Credit seems to be in the most favorable position to accomplish this goal. The expanded functions of this Office fit these purposes, and the prestige of the American Council on Education would encourage many new pioneers.

It is vitally important for the accrediting associations to deal with the same type of broad guidelines. The practice is now widespread enough so that guidance is needed from both regional and professional accrediting bodies. Implicit approval by not condemning the process is no longer sufficient. The accrediting associations owe it to their constituents to consider openly and honestly the crediting of prior learning. One of the leaders in this effort should be the newly formed Council of Postsecondary Accreditation. Resulting from a merger of the Federation of Regional Accrediting Commissions of Higher Education and the National Commission on Accrediting, this Council is intended to "foster and facilitate the roles of non-governmental institutional and specialized agencies in promoting and insuring the quality and diversity of American higher education. It coordinates and periodically reviews the work of its member accrediting agencies, determines the appropriateness of the existing and proposed accrediting activities, and performs other related functions" (*Chronicle of Higher Education*, 1974). With this merger, the new Council becomes the national voice of accreditation and can be most influential in suggesting broad philosophical and operational guidelines for the assessment of prior learning. One of the most pronounced problems is that there is virtually no communication among the various institutions and programs either already involved or about to participate. Some mininetworks of specialized programs touch tangentially on the process, but they tend to be somewhat parochial and spend most of their time and energy speaking to one another. For example, the Union of Experimenting Colleges publishes a newsletter which is circulated among less than fifty University Without Walls programs. The Society for Field Experience, while primarily concerned with future-directed internships, has contemplated prior learning but, again, it has a small, limited audience. Regional higher education consortia, such as the Southern Regional Education Board (SREB), the Western Interstate Commission on Higher Education (WICHE), and the New England Board of Higher Education (NEBHE), have some knowledge about the practice but have not yet made a concerted effort to disseminate this information. State governing boards and commissions of higher education are becoming knowledgeable but their clientele is limited by state boundaries. In addition, these agencies are much more informed about the public sector of higher education within their states than about what is happening at the private institutions.

Two fledgling operations have the potential to become clearinghouses for information on crediting prior learning itself and on which institutions and programs have had experience with the process. The major problem with both is that their concerns go beyond prior learning. The Cooperative Assessment of Experiential Learning (CAEL) Project described earlier is beginning to disseminate information to its General Assembly through a newsletter and through a number of projected conferences. Although this project has responsibility for the entire spectrum of experiential education, it is focusing in on certain difficult aspects of prior learning. The other project, specifically designed as a clearinghouse for all that is new in higher education, is Nexus, of the American Association for Higher Education. A telephone referral service, Nexus links people who have questions about whatever is new in higher education to those people with expertise in the requested area. While Nexus responded to approximately 500 calls from January to June 1974, obviously the crediting of prior learning constitutes only a portion of its emphasis.

The problem of poor communication is associated with the dearth of literature, training materials, and faculty training techniques. Every faculty member interviewed was asked whether he/she thought a training program would be useful. All agreed that it would, regardless of how long they had been involved in crediting. Some individual programs have developed both counseling and faculty evaluation video tapes, but these are used locally and have received little national attention even though the need for this kind of training material is great.

A national center for the assessment of prior learning definitely is needed. Such a center should be independent of established testing bureaus, accrediting associations, and any other agencies which have a vested interest. Although such a center might be attached to a university, it probably would be more beneficial if it were totally independent or under the auspices of one of the national education associations. Functions of such a center would be to: (1) act as a clearinghouse; (2) offer training in crediting prior learning to faculty and administrators, both at the center and in the field; (3) develop training materials such as video and audio tapes, pamphlets, model student portfolios—especially student narratives—and specific guidelines for use by third-party examiners; (4) analyze cost data for the process and (5) engage in an active research program.

Such institutional, regional, and national activities are only beginnings. I also fervently hope that this book is a beginning. A process as new as awarding credit for noncollege learning must not be stifled by *one version of the truth*. The door is now open for a variety of legitimate practices which must be tried out and shared.

⅄⅄⅄ƙƙƙ

Institutions and Programs

The institutions below are those from which written guidelines were received; a complete list of institutions engaged in the practice of crediting prior learning is not available. The people listed with each institution were those most helpful to me in correspondence and during visits. But I suggest that the program rather than the individual be addressed when writing for information.

INSTITUTION	NAME OF SPECIAL PROGRAM	LOCATION	CONTACT PERSON
Adelphi Univ.	ABLE Program	Garden City, N.Y.	Doris Silberstein
²Calif. St. Univ., Dominguez Hills	Small College Program	Dominguez Hills, Calif.	Robert Bersi
¹Calif. St. Univ., San Francisco	External Experience for General Studies Credit	San Francisco, Calif.	Urban Whitaker
Central Michigan Univ.	Institute for Personal & Career Development	Mt. Pleasant, Mich.	Earl Mills
College of St. Benedict	Center for Continuing Education	St. Joseph, Mich.	Kathleen Kalinowski
²College of New Rochelle	New Resources Program	New Rochelle, N.Y.	Joseph McDermott
College of White Plains	Liberal Studies Program	White Plains, N.Y.	Mary Berchmans
CUNY, Brooklyn College	Special Baccalaureate Degree Program for Adults	Brooklyn, N.Y.	John D. Quinn
¹CUNY, Queens College	A.C.E. Program	Flushing, N.Y.	Ernest Schwarcz
²CUNY, University Center	CUNY BA Program	New York City	Sheila Kaplan
²Edison College	——————	Trenton, N.J.	James Brown
Elizabethtown College	Center for Community Education	Elizabethtown, Pa.	James Berkebile
¹Empire St. College	——————	Saratoga, N.Y.	Albert Serling
¹Empire St. College (L. I. Learning Center)	——————	Old Westbury, N.Y.	Ronald Corwin
²Evergreen St. College	Office of External Credit	Olympia, Wash.	Lynn Patterson
¹Florida International Univ.	External Degree Program	Miami, Fla.	Dabney Park
¹Fordham Univ.	EXCEL Program	New York City	Ully Hirsch
Framingham St. College	External Degree Program	Framingham, Mass.	Joseph Palladino
Goddard College	Adult Degree Program	Plainfield, Vt.	John Turner
Hofstra Univ.	U.W.W.	Hempstead, N.Y.	Howard Lord
Iona College	Div. of Gen. Studies	New Rochelle, N.Y.	Elaine Klein

INSTITUTION	NAME OF SPECIAL PROGRAM	LOCATION	CONTACT PERSON
[1]Kansas City, Kansas, Community College	College Without Walls	Kansas City, Kans.	Alton Davies
Lincoln Open Univ.		Naperville, Ill.	Barbara Lowther
[1]Loretto Heights College	U.W.W.	Denver, Colo.	Elinor Greenberg
Marymount College	Continuing Education Program		
[1]Minnesota Metropolitan St. College	Non-Traditional Studies	Tarrytown, N.Y.	Brigid Driscoll
Moorehead St. College	College of Univ. Studies	St. Paul, Minn.	Annie Bell Calhoun
North Dakota St. Univ.	Performance Based Education Project	Moorehead, Minn.	Catherine Warrick
Northern Montana College	Bachelor of Professional Studies Program	Fargo, N.D.	Neil Jacobsen
Pace Univ.		Havre, Mont.	A. W. Korb
Ramapo College	Adult Education	New York City	Geoffrey Needler
Skidmore College	U.W.W.	Ramapo, N.J.	Martha Sachs
Sterling College	Competency Based Curriculum Program	Saratoga, N.Y.	Mark Gelber
[2]Univ. of Mass., Amherst	U.W.W.	Sterling, Kans.	Carol Gene Brownlee
Univ. of Mass., Boston	College of Public and Community Services	Amherst, Mass.	Edward Harris
[1]Univ. of Wis., Green Bay	Community Education Program	Boston, Mass.	Herrick Chapman
[2]Univ. of Wis., Milwaukee		Green Bay, Wis.	Henry Spille
Webster College	Contract Center	Milwaukee, Wis.	Lorraine Fowler
		St. Louis, Mo.	Mary Berchmans

[1] Institutions visited—formal interviews held with students, faculty, and administrators.
[2] Institutions visited—formal and informal interviews held with administrators and/or faculty.

❧❧❧❧❧❧

Bibliography

Though there is a dearth of literature that pertains directly to the practical aspects of awarding credit for non-college learning, the works listed below proved extremely helpful in discussing the need and rationale for crediting prior learning and in presenting regional and national concerns. Those marked with an asterisk are highlighted because of their especially thoughtful treatment of the above. The reader who desires specific information on the practical application of the process should write directly to the institutions and programs listed in the previous chapter.

187

*American Council on Education. "Expansion of Activities of the Commission on Accreditation of Service Experiences of the American Council on Education." Paper prepared for Board of Directors. Washington, D. C.: American Council on Education, 1974. Duplicated.

BOYER, E. L. "Higher Education: Breaking Up the Youth Ghetto." Address presented at the 29th National Conference on Higher Education. Washington, D. C.: American Association for Higher Education, 1974.

BUTTS, R. F. A Cultural History of Western Education. Second edition. New York: McGraw-Hill, 1955.

*The Carnegie Commission on Higher Education. Less Time, More Options. Highstown, N. J.: McGraw-Hill, 1971.

The Carnegie Commission on Higher Education. Reform on Campus. Highstown, N. J.: McGraw-Hill, 1972.

The Chronicle of Higher Education, 1974 8(10), 12.

*The Commission on Non-Traditional Study. Diversity By Design. San Francisco: Jossey-Bass, 1973.

*CROSS, K. P., VALLEY, J. R., AND ASSOCIATES. Planning Non-Traditional Programs. San Francisco: Jossey-Bass, 1974.

*Educational Testing Service. "CAEL: Cooperative Assessment of Experiential Learning." Condensed version of a proposal. Princeton, N. J.: Educational Testing Service, 1973. Duplicated.

ELBOW, P. "Shall We Teach Or Give Credit? A Model for Higher Education." Soundings, Fall 1971.

Federation of Regional Accrediting Commissions of Higher Education. "Interim Statement on Accreditation and Non-Traditional Study." Washington, D. C.: FRACHE, 1973.

The General Assembly of Pennsylvania. "Senate Bill No. 1472, Session of 1974." Harrisburg: The General Assembly of Pennsylvania, 1974.

*GOULD, S. B., AND CROSS, K. P. (Eds.) Explorations in Non-Traditional Study. San Francisco: Jossey-Bass, 1972.

HARRIS, J. "Baccalaureate Requirements: Attainments or Exposures?" Educational Record, Winter 1972, 59–65.

HODGKINSON, H. L. "Regional Examining Institutes." Address presented at the 29th National Conference on Higher Education. Washington, D. C.: American Association for Higher Education, 1974.

HYNES, R. Untitled address to the Southern Association of Colleges and Schools, 1973.

LONDON, P. "The Psychotherapy Boom: From the Long Couch for the Sick to the Push Button for the Bored." *Psychology Today*, 1974, *8* (1), 63–68.

MEDSKER, L. L. "Abstract: The Assessment of New Institutional Forms for Extending Postsecondary Education." Berkeley: Center for Research and Development in Higher Education, University of California, Berkeley, 1974. Duplicated.

MEYER, P. "The Evening College: A Question of Responsibility." Address delivered to the International Association of Evening Student Councils. Flushing, N. Y.: Queens College, 1965.

MEYER, P., AND PETRY, S. L. *Off-Campus Education: An Inquiry.* Atlanta, Ga.: Southern Regional Education Board, 1972.

Michigan State Board of Education, "Issue Paper on the External Degree Program." East Lansing: Michigan State Board of Education, 1973. Duplicated.

MILLER, J. W. "Credentialing for Health Administration." Address delivered to the Commission for Health Administration, 1973.

MILLER, J. W. *Organizational Structure of Nongovernmental Postsecondary Accreditation: Relationship to Uses of Accreditation.* Washington, D. C.: National Commission on Accrediting, 1973.

MULHOLLAND, J. "Notes on the General Problems of Evaluation of Credits for Life Experience." Address delivered at Florida International University, Miami, 1973.

The Planning Task Force, Regents Statewide University, The University of Wisconsin System. "A Planning Prospectus for the Open University of the University of Wisconsin System." Madison: The University of Wisconsin System, 1973. Duplicated.

*The Study on Continuing Education and the Future. *The Learning Society.* Notre Dame, Indiana: The University of Notre Dame, n.d.

TAYLOR, H. *The World As Teacher.* Garden City, N. Y.: Doubleday, 1969.

TAYLOR, H. *How To Change Colleges: Notes on Radical Reform.* New York: Holt, Rinehart and Winston, 1971.

*VERMILYE, D. W. (Ed.) *The Expanded Campus.* Washington, D. C.: American Association for Higher Education, 1972.

꓆꓆꓆꓆꓆꓆

Index

190